FIGHT YOUR WAY
TO A BETTER MARRIAGE

FIGHT YOUR WAY

TO A BETTER MARRIAGE

{
HOW HEALTHY CONFLICT CAN TAKE YOU TO

DEEPER LEVELS OF INTIMACY
}

DR. GREG SMALLEY

HOWARD BOOKS
A DIVISION OF SIMON & SCHUSTER, INC.
New York · Nashville · London · Toronto · Sydney · New Delhi

Howard Books
A Division of Simon & Schuster, Inc.
1230 Avenue of the Americas
New York, NY 10020

First Howard Books hardcover edition November 2012

HOWARD and colophon are trademarks of Simon & Schuster, Inc.

For information about special discounts for bulk purchases, please contact Simon & Schuster Special Sales at 1-866-506-1949 or business@simonandschuster.com.

The Simon & Schuster Speakers Bureau can bring authors to your live event. For more information or to book an event, contact the Simon & Schuster Speakers Bureau at 1-866-248-3049 or visit our website at www.simonspeakers.com.

Manufactured in the United States of America

10   9   8   7   6   5   4   3   2   1

Library of Congress Cataloging-in-Publication Data
Smalley, Greg.
   Fight your way to a better marriage : how conflict can take you to deeper levels of intimacy / by Greg Smalley.
      p. cm.
1. Marriage—Religious aspects—Christianity. 2. Conflict management—Religious aspects—Christianity. 3. Interpersonal relations—Religious aspects—Christianity. 4. Man-woman relationships—Religious aspects—Christianity. I. Title.
   BV835.S5556 2012
   248.8'44—dc23
                                        2012016884

ISBN 978-1-4165-4483-8
ISBN 978-1-4516-6920-6 (ebook)

To my wife and best friend, Erin,
thank you for always fighting for our marriage.
I love you with all my heart.

To Gary J. Oliver, thank you
for teaching me how conflict provides such amazing
opportunities for growth in a relationship.

Contents

~~~~~~~~~~~~~~~~~~~~~~~~~~~~~~~

One

The Power of Healthy Conflict

Your marriage needs conflict.

And yet, sadly, people rarely believe this. It's probably because conflict is a topic that makes many of us feel uncomfortable. It can bring fear to our hearts and remind us of past failures and acts of which we are ashamed. Our lives are pockmarked by battles and arguments with our loved ones, like the one I experienced while returning from a date night with my wife.

"You're speeding," Erin warned.

"I'm driving the speed limit," I snapped. "Quit trying to control me."

"I'm telling you that the speed limit is thirty-five," Erin shot back, "and you're doing forty-five. You're going to get a ticket!"

"This is a brand-new road in the middle of nowhere," I argued. "Why would they make it thirty-five? I'm positive that it's forty-five. Besides, why would anyone care if I'm going a little fast on a deserted road?"

Apparently someone cared, as evidenced by the blue and red lights flashing behind me.

Difficulties are meant to rouse, not discourage.
The human spirit is to grow strong by conflict.

—WILLIAM ELLERY CHANNING

And before I could give her that look that says, "Don't you dare," Erin gloated, "I warned you. But maybe you'll learn to believe me after our insurance rates go up."

This was one of those moments when I desperately wanted to run far away from my wife, but I figured that fleeing my vehicle might present a whole new set of problems for me.

As the officer approached my window, he asked the one question that I was hoping he wouldn't: "Do you know how fast you were going?"

Haven't you ever wanted to smart off by saying something like "No . . . it's really difficult to see over the beer can," or "I don't, but I bet you do!" I'm so glad I only think these things and don't say them out loud.

Well, before I could actually say "No, kind sir, I don't know how fast I was going" in my politest voice, Erin snapped, "He knows. I told him he was speeding, but he chose not to listen."

Ouch.

To make matters worse, the officer said, "So you don't know how fast you were going. I guess that means I can write anything I want on the ticket, huh?"

Again . . . *ouch!* Who were these two, a comedy team?

I probably should have stopped there, but I thought that after the drubbing I'd received from my wife and the officer, he'd have compassion for me.

"Any way you'd let me off with a warning?" I begged. "The real punishment will be having to endure the 'I told you so' all the way home. A ticket would be over the top—like beating a dead horse."

When will I learn that some people don't find me funny?

"You want a warning?" the officer said graciously. "Okay, I'm warning you that if you go above the speed limit again, I'll give you *another* ticket."

With that, I was done. Unfortunately, Erin wasn't finished. After she directed some additional choice words and phrases at me, we spent the rest of the drive home in silence.

You may be wondering, "How could an interaction like that be something my marriage needs?" Let me explain.

CONFLICT: BEAUTY OR THE BEAST?

What images come into your mind when you think about conflict? Perhaps you fought with your parents, kids in the neighborhood, school bullies, friends in junior high, or teachers. Maybe your marriage is riddled with conflict today, or perhaps you never fight. Whatever your past or current experiences, how do you perceive conflict? Are these images positive or negative? Conflict has the potential for beauty, but at the same time, there is also a "beast" lurking in it if we mishandle our conflicts.

In an *unhealthy* sense, if we avoid conflict, pretend it doesn't exist, gossip to others about it, get angry, or intimidate others into doing what we want, the greater the problem will become, and the greater the relational damage will be. Couples who do not work out their differences and manage their conflict issues are at risk for divorce.

The apostle Paul recognized this when he wrote, "If you keep on biting and devouring each other, watch out or you will be destroyed by each other" (Galatians 5:15).

Many couples hate to confront disagreements and hurts because they're afraid of rocking the boat, so they choose to keep the peace at any price and sweep their issues under the rug. However, this strategy usually does not resolve the problem, because suppressed conflict is always buried alive, and it often festers until it becomes a much bigger problem. In the end, buried issues end up exploding like a massive volcano, leaving our spouse and family members in its wake of destruction. Dallin H. Oaks said, "Peace . . . is not just the absence of war. It's the opposite of war."[1]

In Matthew 5:23–24 we are encouraged to deal with relationship problems so that our hearts will be right when we worship the Lord. "Therefore, if you are offering your gift at the altar and there remember that your brother has something against you, leave your gift there in front of the altar. First go and be reconciled to your brother; then come and offer your gift."

The difficulty with mishandled conflict is that it creates an unsafe environment. Spouses feel like they are walking on a thin layer of volcanic crust, while underneath rages a river of molten lava ready to consume those trapped nearby. And when people feel unsafe, their heart closes and they disconnect. This is why, when asked about divorce, Jesus said, "Moses permitted you to divorce your wives because your hearts were hard" (Matthew 19:8). A hard heart is the kiss of death to a marriage, and that is exactly what prolonged, unhealthy conflict creates: *a hardened heart*! King Solomon deeply understood the reality of a hard heart: "An offended friend is harder to win back than a fortified city. Arguments separate friends like a gate locked with bars" (Proverbs 18:19). Indeed, not confronting and managing conflict often causes long-term resentment, which eventually destroys feelings of love in a marriage. The bottom line is your marriage may not last if you do not work through issues. This is why two of the world's top marriage experts, Scott Stanley and Howard Markman, claim that managing conflict is the key to staying in love and staying married. Their thirty years of research indicate that if couples learned to work out their conflicts, the overall divorce rate could be cut by over 50 percent.[2]

No pressure, no diamonds.

—MARY CASE

That's amazing! Who knew that actually facing our differences and managing our conflict in a healthy way could produce such results? It's true that conflict can be a beast, but there also exists a beauty. I love marital-art master Thomas Crum's image of conflict:

One of the myths is the idea that conflict is negative. . . . Nature doesn't see conflict as a negative. Nature uses conflict as a primary motivator for change. Imagine floating down the Colorado River through the Grand Canyon. Quiet water flowing into exhilarating rapids. Hidden canyons with shade trees and wildflowers. Clear springs of drinkable water. Solitude and silence that can be found in few places in today's world. And those majestic cliffs looming above, with fantastic patterns in the rock and all the colors of the rainbow displayed. The Grand Canyon is truly one of the world's greatest wonders and provides us with a profound sense of harmony and peace. Yet how was that amazing vista formed? Eons and eons of water flowing, continually wearing away the rock, carrying it to the sea. A conflict that continues to this day. Conflict isn't negative, it just is.[3]

Let's face it, unless you're a black belt like Thomas Crum, few people are genuinely excited about conflict. And yet it's essential that we recognize conflict for what it is: an unavoidable and potentially beneficial part of being in a relationship with another human being.

Let me explain these two truths about conflict. First, conflict is inevitable. Any person involved in a sustained relationship is bound to experience conflict with that other person eventually. It's a part of getting to know and adjusting to a person, his or her habits, values, and ways of functioning. Two people will never have the same expectations, thoughts, opinions, or needs. In fact, marriage expert Dr. Larry Nadig believes that a relationship with no apparent conflict may be unhealthier than one with frequent conflict.[4]

Absence of conflict suggests the presence of deadened emotions or a hardened heart, or that one spouse is being suppressed or giving in to his or her mate. This might be acceptable over the short term, but over the long term, it's very dangerous to the marriage. Anger is likely to build to the point where the conflict, when it surfaces, will be more intense than it needed to be. Second, although conflict is unavoidable, it can also bring amazing benefits to a relationship. Watch how this happens.

THE HIDDEN VALUE OF CONFLICT

Few people know that Murfreesboro, Arkansas, is home to Crater of Diamonds State Park, the only diamond-producing site in the world where the public can search for diamonds. For a small fee, visitors can dig for diamonds and keep whatever they find.

The park is located above the eroded surface of an ancient volcanic pipe. This "crater" is actually a thirty-seven-acre open field that is plowed from time to time to bring diamonds and other gemstones to the surface. I will never forget my first impression of this place. It wasn't pretty. What they don't tell you in their lovely brochure is that the volcanic field (don't forget the eroded part) is a treeless wasteland of dirt and rocks and, apparently, diamonds. At first glance, it seems impossible that there could be anything valuable hidden beneath the ancient volcanic dirt. This is actually a perfect picture of the hidden value of conflict. On the surface, conflict is not pretty. For some, it feels rocky and treacherous—full of tension and anger. Other couples experience conflict more as a distant wasteland—filled with avoidance and withdrawal. Either way, most couples experience conflict as frustrating and painful, something they should definitely avoid. However, as the person who found a 40.23-carat diamond at the state park discovered, conflict is loaded with potential treasures as well.

Conflict is inevitable, but combat is optional.

—MAX LUCADO

I know it may be hard to believe, but there really is something amazing about conflict. Yet most people, for good reason, view conflict in a negative light. They believe that the arguments and angry interactions between a husband and wife are not just stressful but unhealthy. In the end, many couples see conflict as a sign that their relationship is in trouble. This belief is understandable yet unfortunate. Conflict is not negative; instead, it's an inevitable part of marriage that will be managed in either a healthy or an unhealthy way. I prefer the word "managing" over "resolving" conflicts. Rather than making it our goal to resolve arguments, we must learn how to manage conflict. Research suggests that 31 percent of couples' major continuing disagreements are about resolvable issues. However, 69 percent are about unresolvable perpetual problems that never get resolved but must be managed.[5]

The good news is that if we manage conflict in a healthy way, like Crater of Diamonds State Park, it is loaded with treasures to be unearthed. Marriage expert John Gottman agrees:

If there is one lesson I have learned from my years of research it is that a lasting marriage results from a couple's ability to resolve the conflicts that are inevitable in any relationship. Many couples tend to equate a low level of conflict with happiness and believe the claim "we never fight" is a sign of marital health. But I believe we grow in our relationships by reconciling our differences. That's how we become more loving people and truly experience the fruits of marriage.[6]

Satisfied couples are more likely to discuss issues of disagreement, whereas dissatisfied couples are more likely to minimize or avoid conflict.

This is exactly what Jesus was talking about when he said, "If your brother sins against you, go and show him his fault, just between the two of you. If he listens to you, you have won your brother over" (Matthew 18:15).

In the same way that the Grand Canyon expands as the Colorado River fights its way through, *healthy* conflict helps a marriage to grow and evolve. If handled right, arguments have the potential to create greater understanding, trust, and connection. You can literally "win your spouse over." Many people fail to see the true value of disagreement because it's housed in something unpleasant and unglamorous—like that wasteland of ancient volcanic dirt. Most couples fail to notice the diamonds lying just under the surface, waiting to be discovered. Here are a few of the diamonds buried within healthy conflict:

- Brings problems into the light and helps couples face their issues instead of denying or avoiding them
- Helps you to better appreciate the differences between you and your spouse
- Gives you a chance to care for and empathize with your spouse
- Provides an opportunity to break old, ineffective patterns
- Can restore unity and oneness
- Humbles us and God gives his grace to the humble (James 4:6)
- Gives you great insight into your own personal issues
- Helps you learn how to anticipate and resolve future conflicts
- Brings you closer together as you listen, understand, and validate each other
- Provides a great source of information. For example, conflict can reveal the need to spend more time together
- Can raise you to higher levels of marital satisfaction every time you manage the conflict well
- Is the sole reason we have the amazing experience of make-up sex

Isn't this a great list of what conflict can do if we learn to walk through it in a healthy way? As the prophet Isaiah put it, "to bestow on them a crow of beauty instead of ashes" (Isaiah 61:3).

So what is the real value of conflict? If we compared each potential conflict benefit on that previous list to a 2-carat diamond, the most valuable aspect of relational disagreements would be like the 40-carat diamond discovered at the Crater of Diamonds State Park. Here is the real value of conflict.

Fear not those who argue but those who dodge.

—DALE CARNEGIE

THE DOORWAY TO INTIMACY

Conflict and arguments have the ability to strengthen or deteriorate a marriage relationship. On one hand, healthy conflict can facilitate deeper understanding, trust, connection and respect—true intimacy. On the other hand, arguments can be unhealthy, causing frustration, hurt, disconnection, and hardened hearts. As Larry Nadig puts it, "How the conflicts are managed, not how many occur, is the critical factor in determining whether your relationship will be healthy or unhealthy, mutually satisfying or unsatisfying, friendly or unfriendly, deep or shallow, intimate or cold."[7]

The reality is that a conflict like the one I had with my wife when I was speeding doesn't guarantee intimacy; it only provides a foundation where deep connection *can* occur. That doesn't mean we keep fighting just so we can enjoy the deeper intimacy of making up. But when a conflict does occur, it can bring an amazing benefit (like a

40-carat diamond) if we use it in the right way. I know this is hard to believe, but it's true: Conflict provides the opportunity to deepen your understanding of your spouse. This is the real treasure. Notice I said the *opportunity* for intimacy. Marriage expert John Gottman expresses this same sentiment:

> The idea that conflict is healthy may sound like a cruel joke if you're feeling overwhelmed by the negativity in your relationship. But in a sense, a relationship lives and dies by what you might loosely call its arguments, by how well disagreements and grievances are aired. The key is how you argue— whether your style escalates tension or leads to a feeling of resolution.[8]

You and your spouse are different in some amazing ways, which is one of the many reasons your marriage is so valuable. However, people often associate their differences as the cause of their marriage problems. And yet this isn't true. The evil one wants you to view your differences as the problem. But the truth is that your differences aren't the problem; it's how you *manage* your differences. The conflict around your differences is the real culprit for frustration and heartache in your marriage. Most of us ultimately view conflict as something to avoid rather than something that can be used to help us better understand each other. As noted marriage expert Gary J. Oliver explains, "The real problem isn't that we are different or that we disagree and experience conflict. The real problem is that most of us automatically view conflict as negative rather than as a tool that God can use to help us better understand ourselves and each other."[9]

The most important thing for a good marriage is to learn how to argue peaceably.

—ANITA EKBERG

Healthy conflict is the entryway to better understanding our spouse. The moment we get into an argument, there is that open door to discover our spouse's most important feelings and needs. Instead of reverting to old patterns of reaction when our buttons get pushed, our mind-set should be "I'm thankful for this disagreement because it gives us an opportunity to deepen our understanding and intimacy." Doesn't this sound like 1 Thessalonians 5:18, "Give thanks in all circumstances, for this is God's will for you in Christ Jesus?" This is how we strengthen our relationship through conflict.

Let me illustrate how this doorway of intimacy works. After Erin and I returned home from our date where I got the ticket for speeding, I felt like the old Bobby Fuller Four song "I Fought the Law and the Law Won." As we walked into our house, we weren't speaking to each other and were disconnected, to say the least. I must admit it didn't seem like much of a doorway; it felt more like a stone wall.

Later that night, I approached Erin in our bedroom.

"I know I acted like an idiot tonight," I said softly. "Would you forgive me?"

"Absolutely," she responded. "But why did you get so defensive? I want to know what was really going on." She is so wise. I completely understand why King Solomon wrote, "A man's greatest treasure is his wife. She is a gift from the Lord" (Proverbs 18:22).

As we talked openly about the driving incident, I was able to better understand that Erin felt invalidated when I wasn't open to her concern about speeding: "I knew that the speed limit was thirty-five, but I felt extremely marginalized." She helped me understand that when I dismiss her opinions, she feels devalued and disconnected. I was able to help Erin understand that when she criticizes my driving, I feel controlled and disrespected. To make matters worse, once I got pulled over by the police, I felt as if I had failed. "Feeling like a failure is a huge issue for me," I explained. "I quickly shut down when I feel like I failed." Deeply listening to, understanding, and validating each other's feelings is an enormous treasure for our marriage.

Going even deeper through the doorway, conflict can take us past simply talking about our feelings (which is good) all the way to discussing the core of what we really want and need from each other (which is great). Erin wants me to be open to accepting her influence when she shares a concern, instead of outright dismissing her or marginalizing her feedback. It helps her feel loved when I listen and communicate to her that I'm taking her concerns seriously and considering them. As a matter of fact, since that time, I've learned to say in all seriousness, "I'll pray about what you just shared and then get back to you."

John Gottman says that marriage succeeds to the extent that the husband accepts influence from his wife: "A husband's ability to be influenced by his wife (rather than vice versa) is crucial because research shows women are already well practiced at accepting influence from men, and a true partnership occurs only when a husband can do so as well."[10]

These researchers are killing my ego!

*Conflict isn't good or bad, right or wrong . . . conflict
simply is. It is how we choose to respond to conflict
that produces the growth or creates the real problem.*

—GARY J. OLIVER

That night I was able to help Erin understand that it would help
if, before correcting my driving, she would consider whether she
was being critical or sharing a concern. Sometimes her words, tone,
and facial expressions communicate criticism. I also shared that I
feel like she rubs it in my face when I make a mistake or when she is
right (which is often). I disconnect or log off pretty fast when I feel
piled on by her.

Certainly we didn't handle the beginning of the argument in the
car very well. Some might even suggest that it was rather unhealthy.
And yet what matters most is not how you begin but how you end.
Ultimately, we walked through that doorway and discovered several
relational diamonds. This is something that I've learned over and
over in my marriage: When conflict is managed in a healthy way,
people feel safe to open their heart and reveal who they really are.
They feel open to display their uniqueness and opinions and to share
their concerns, hurts, fears, and frustrations. This is why conflict is
a doorway to intimacy and why your marriage needs conflict. This is
exactly what my dad, Gary Smalley, explained as well:

Conflict is inevitable in relationships. It rears its head in even
the healthiest, most deeply intimate of marriages. It is how you
handle conflict that will determine how it affects your relationship, for better or for worse. Again, the most important aspect

is not how much you love each other or how committed you
are to your relationship or the strength of your faith; optimum
relationships depend on how adeptly you handle conflict. Every instance of conflict represents two divergent paths: you
can use it to either grow together or grow apart. Open the
door. Walk through—and you learn more about the delights
of marriage than you ever dreamed possible.[11]

I love that thought: We can use conflict to grow either closer together or further apart. I hope you see that tapping in to the power
of healthy conflict is a matter of opening the door, not closing it.
Sometimes I want to slam the conflict door shut and lock it when I
know Erin has an issue with me. But look at the growth opportunities I'd be missing out on. You have the same choice. You can either
return to old patterns of dealing with conflict or walk through the
doorway of healthy conflict and into the deepest levels of intimacy
and connection, to the place Peter envisioned for our relationships:
"Love each other deeply from the heart" (1 Peter 1:22). The choice
is yours!

Before I continue, I want to be perfectly clear about the intended
audience for this book. *Fight Your Way to a Better Marriage* is for those
who struggle with common conflict issues that prevent them from
reaching the deepest levels of intimacy and connection. It is not intended for anyone in an abusive marriage. When I talk about "unhealthy" conflict, I am not referring to abuse (intense or extreme
degrading language, intimidation, shoving, slapping, hitting, threats
of violence, raging, forced sex, etc.). If these types of destructive behaviors are present within your marriage, I would never recommend
putting yourself or other family members in danger by remaining
in an abusive environment. Instead, safety is your primary concern,
and I would recommend that you get help immediately from the

police, a professionally trained counselor, or the National Domestic Violence Hotline (800-799-7233).

Within the pages of this book, I will teach you how to turn your everyday conflicts into healthy conflict so your marriage can reap the amazing benefits. We will begin by looking into what is at the heart of every conflict—in other words, what drives every single experience when you get hurt by or frustrated at your spouse. It has everything to do with the fact that people push your buttons and then you react. This creates a nasty relationship cycle that closes your heart and keeps you stuck in a pattern of unhealthy conflict. You will discover how your buttons are really lies that have been written on your heart. Then I'll show you how to heal your heart through God's truth. Finally, you will learn the power of working together to find solutions as teammates—decisions that both people feel great about.

Next, we will examine what to do, in a practical manner, when your buttons get pushed. Then we will focus on how to create the right environment for you to have a productive discussion with your spouse. I'll also show you the greatest communication method that I know, called L.U.V.E. talk, to help you and your spouse reach the deepest levels of intimacy and connection after any argument.

More than anything, I want to show you a process of working through every problem that you will face. My goal is not to solve specific problems; instead, I want to offer you a step-by-step system of managing conflict in a healthy way. Ultimately, I want to help you understand your spouse's deepest needs. One of the best opportunities is through conflict. The essence of this book is *learning to make conflict work for you rather than against you.* I want to help you "fight" your way to a better marriage.

Two

The Reactive Cycle

Do you ever experience moments when something happens that pushes your buttons, as the saying goes? You know, when something happens that leaves you feeling annoyed, frustrated, hurt, upset, or even angry? Maybe it's one of these situations:

- The drive-through line is too long at your favorite coffee place or fast-food restaurant.
- You wake up to dirty dishes in the sink.
- Your favorite TV show or game didn't record.
- There's a long wait at the doctor's office.
- Someone cuts in line.
- Your child tracks mud or spills something on your clean floor.
- A driver tailgates.

I don't know about you, but I'm feeling riled up just reading through this list!

Of course, the list is nothing compared to the fury that arguments with our spouses can arouse in us. Why is it that we so often say something or behave in ways that we end up regretting—that seem out of character? It's like we start acting out of the same script time after time, as if we're spinning around in the same ridiculous cycle, ending up frustrated, hurt, angry, or emotionally hijacked. Why do we do this? The answer is actually quite simple. Every frustration, every hurt feeling, every heated argument, every negative approach to conflict is triggered by one thing: the Reactive Cycle. Watch how this works.

"I told you the hotel warned us!" Erin stated firmly as she handed me the "Warning/Danger" memo.

I didn't even know people still used the word "memo." But before I could look at the document, Erin grabbed it again and started reading in that "I told you" voice. You know the one I'm talking about, right? It's the one where the confident and clearly wounded spouse emphasizes every incriminating word to further prove your guilt. *That* voice.

Erin scanned the memo until she apparently found the most damaging evidence. "Here it is," she reprimanded, " 'a storm surge is water pushed toward the shore by the force of the winds swirling around the storm. This advancing surge combines with the normal tides to create a hurricane' "—she paused at the word "hurricane"— " 'storm tide, which can increase the water level fifteen feet or more. This rise in water level can cause severe flooding in coastal areas, particularly when the storm tide coincides with the normal high tides.' "

I was speechless.

"This is why I told you not to take our babies"—our children were fourteen, eleven, and seven at the time—"to the beach, and why I specifically asked you not to let them swim in the hurricane waves during high tide."

How did she know it was high tide?

"Don't you think the word 'hurricane' is a little melodramatic?" I countered. When will I ever learn?

"Forget the fact that you almost killed our children," Erin yelled as she slammed the bathroom door closed, "you completely dishonored me in front of your family." And then she was gone.

Since I never got to properly defend myself to Erin, let me tell you what happened.

You see, we were visiting my brother and his family in Houston. As part of the reunion, we stayed a couple of nights in Corpus Christi at a beach resort. Upon arriving in this postcard perfect beachfront hotel, we were shocked to discover that a tropical storm (notice I said tropical storm and not "hurricane") was approaching. Apparently, the hotel sent out a memo warning the guests about the dangers of swimming during the storm—who knew?

That afternoon I took the kids down to the beach so we could build sand castles. (By the way, I now completely understand the parable of the man who built his house upon the sand!) Try erecting a sand castle during a surging tropical storm with gale-force winds. It really brings Matthew 7:26–27 to life: "But everyone who hears these words of mine and does not put them into practice is like a foolish man who built his house on sand. The rain came down, the streams rose, and the winds blew and beat against that house, and it fell with a great crash."

Once I realized that building a sand castle in the midst of a wind-blown storm surge probably wasn't the best idea, I switched to a more reasonable plan. I challenged my kids to see who could body-surf the biggest wave! I know what you're thinking: "Why am I taking any advice from this guy?" Fair enough. But I never said this was a book about parenting.

After watching my children (certainly not babies) being slammed onto the sand by some enormous waves, I thought we should probably move our contest to the swimming pool. I reasoned there was less chance that they would break something. See? I can be responsible.

Ironically, Erin arrived at the pool about the same time we cannonballed into the Jacuzzi. By that time I was extremely tired and hungry from battling the surging water, the giant waves, and the blowing sand, so I asked my family if they wanted to eat. Basically, everyone ignored me. Knowing that our children were in safe hands with my nearly fourteen-year-old nephew, I left them playing in the water while I searched for some food. I also knew that Erin was nearby.

After raiding the snack bar, I joined my brother and his family to eat lunch. My brother and I quickly found ourselves engrossed in deep conversation about . . . well, I don't remember exactly what we were talking about, but I'm sure it had something to do with our immense love for our wives or some pressing spiritual concern. Okay, it might have been about sports. The point was that I was enjoying the conversation. It was at this exact moment that Erin walked up and said, "The kids are all playing in the pool with your young nephew, which doesn't make me feel very safe. Will you go watch them?"

Marriage is nature's way of keeping people from fighting with strangers.

—AUTHOR UNKNOWN

I wanted to say, "If *that* doesn't make you feel safe, you should have watched us building sand castles and bodysurfing the massive waves!" Thankfully, I only thought it.

Here is where Erin and I perceive things differently. I understood her to have asked me a question: "Will you go watch them?" Notice the word "will" and the question mark at the end. When someone asks you a question, "no" is supposed to be a perfectly acceptable option; otherwise, it's not a question but a demand.

Erin doesn't remember our exchange quite the same way.

Nonetheless, I was deep in conversation with my brother, so I answered, "Not really."

This was one of those times between a husband and a wife when words aren't necessary. The look I received made the old cliché about a picture being worth a thousand words seem like a massive understatement.

I took offense at her heart-piercing look, so I may have uttered one or two sarcastic comments in return. I don't think I did, but it is possible—at least that's what she claims.

Needless to say, Erin and I engaged in a quick round of allegations, accusations, defensiveness, sarcasm, and I may have made some reference about her mother, but I'm not sure. However, it's never a good sign when someone's mother gets brought into the conversation.

The impressive part of our entire exchange was that it was done in whisper mode. You know whisper mode, don't you? It's when you and your spouse don't want other people to hear what you're arguing about. So you engage in a heated argument, but you try to keep your voices down. Unfortunately, you end up looking like two rabid mimes trying to silently kill each other. Welcome to the Reactive Cycle!

*Life is a cycle, always in motion; if good times have
moved on, so will times of trouble!*

—INDIAN PROVERB

THE REACTIVE CYCLE

What happened to Erin and me in Corpus Christi? How did we go from enjoying a pleasant afternoon at the beach to all-out war by the pool? If I were one of those ESPN play-by-play sports analysts, I'd explain our conflict to the TV audience by drawing the following diagram:

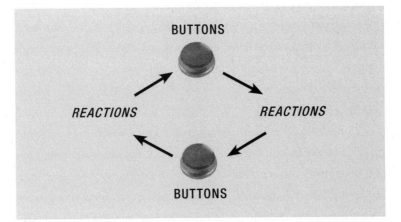

Let me break this illustration down. When your spouse does or says something that hits you wrong, hurts your feelings, frustrates you, or makes you mad, it pushes one of your buttons. As a result, you negatively react in order to deal with the unwanted feelings that go along with having your trigger tripped. You might defend yourself, withdraw, criticize, shut down, get angry, or give the silent treatment, for example. Usually, your reaction pushes your spouse's buttons. Since your spouse doesn't like how it feels, either, she negatively reacts, hoping her reaction will change you or make her feel better. Listen to how author Robert Burney explains the cycle:

In most relationships where the people have been together for a few years they have already established entrenched battle lines around painful emotional scars where they push each other's buttons. All one person has to do is use a certain tone of voice or have a certain look on [his or her] face and the other person pulls out and loads the big guns. One person is readying their answer in their head to what they "know" the other is going to say before the other even has a chance to say it. The battle begins and neither one of them actually listens to what the other is saying. They start pulling out their lists of past hurts to prove their point of how each other is "doing" horrible things to them. The battle is on to see who is right and who is wrong.[1]

This is the Reactive Cycle. It's exactly what Erin and I did at the poolside, and I know that you and your spouse do it as well (although your cycle may look different from ours). We *all* get our buttons pushed multiple times throughout the day, and then we react. It's universal. Unfortunately, the cycle never gets you what you really want—connection, intimacy, understanding, validation, feeling loved, success, and so on. Instead, you and your spouse spin around until the discussion escalates into an angry mess, someone shuts down, or you both withdraw, frustrated and disconnected. Marriage expert John Gottman developed a list that can help you determine whether you're in the throes of the Reactive Cycle:

- The conflict makes you feel rejected by your spouse.
- You keep talking about it but make no headway.
- You become entrenched in your positions and are unwilling to budge.
- When you discuss the subject, you end up feeling more frustrated and hurt.
- Your conversations about the problem are devoid of humor, amusement, or affection.
- You become even more unbudgeable over time, which leads you to vilify each other during these conversations.
- This vilification makes you all the more rooted in your position and polarized, more extreme in your view, and all the less willing to compromise.
- Eventually, you disengage from each other emotionally.[2]

If any of these situations sound painfully familiar, the good news is that there is a way out of this relational gridlock, no matter how stuck you feel. The first step is to explore what gets the cycle spinning: your buttons getting pushed.

EMOTIONAL BUTTONS

I recently read a funny story about a wife's buttons getting pushed in the most embarrassing way. The wife invited several couples over for dinner. It wasn't that her husband didn't like the couples, but he was tired from working late and didn't feel very social that evening.

Truth be told, the last thing the husband wanted was to talk to a bunch of people he hardly knew. I can relate!

Once everyone was seated around the table, the wife turned to their six-year-old daughter and asked, "Would you like to say the blessing?"

"I wouldn't know what to say," the young girl replied.

"Just say what you hear Daddy say," the wife encouraged.

Everyone looked at the husband and then smiled at the girl as they waited for her prayer. The young daughter bowed her head and said: "Dear Lord, why on earth did we invite all these people to dinner?"

Quarrels would not last so long if the fault lay only on one side.

—FRANÇOIS DE LA ROCHEFOUCAULD

Needless to say, several buttons were instantly triggered around the table. I'm sure the young girl felt embarrassed when the dinner guests gasped in the middle of her prayer. The wife probably felt a surge of humiliation at her daughter's candid revelation. The husband may have felt betrayed by his daughter and certainly felt instant pain jolt up his leg from his wife kicking his shin under the table. I'm quite sure the guests felt a myriad of emotions as they pondered the husband's feelings toward them.

When I think about our buttons, I picture one of those "Easy Button" gadgets from Staples that says "That was easy" when you press it. It's like we all have several easy buttons attached to our bodies. J. H. Larson described it this way:

Everyone has "buttons." They're your tender spots, the places where you're most sensitive, the points where you get irritated, or hurt, or angry, and have to react. Buttons are triggered by specific events or circumstances and typically take over and direct your behavior. They also carry a strong emotional charge when they're activated, so that behavior is going to be emotional and extreme. There's nothing rational or considered about a response that comes from a button. It's pure emotion. You'll know you were acting under the influence of a button when you regret what you did or said the moment you cool off. The words just popped out, you turned away and slammed the door behind you. You didn't think about it until afterwards. At the time, it was simply what you had to do. That was a button.[3]

What exactly is a button? Buttons represent sensitive areas or touchy issues that are easily triggered. A button might be a pet peeve. For example, you may become annoyed and react angrily when people leave the toilet lid up or dirty dishes in the sink, and yet you may not feel any irritation whatsoever at a driver going below the speed limit (which makes me crazy—please, when it says 55, go 55!).

I don't have pet peeves, I have whole kernels of irritation.

—WHOOPI GOLDBERG

A button could signify that you are being forced to act in ways that oppose your natural personality strength. For example, if you are a structured person, being asked to be spontaneous may cause you to feel out of control; or if you are used to leading and being in charge, being in a situation that requires you to follow may make you feel powerless.

Fear can be a button as well. "But the LORD God called to the man, 'Where are you?' He answered, 'I heard you in the garden, and I was afraid because I was naked; so I hid'" (Genesis 3:9–10). We fear feeling unloved, failed, rejected, disrespected, and so on. When our fears are triggered, we react, just like Adam did.

Buttons can represent an unmet expectation. One explanation for the current high divorce rate and the prevalence of marital dissatisfaction is that we have high and unrealistic expectations of marriage—expecting a spouse to be simultaneously a friend, a confidant, a fulfilling sex partner, a counselor, and a parent.[4] An expectation is what we anticipate or assume will or won't happen within a relationship. For example, you might expect your spouse to call you during the day, maintain the car, do the yard work, or cook the meals. On the other hand, you may expect that your spouse will not call you at work, never discuss weight issues, and never work on Sunday. When things happen differently than we expected, we go into reaction mode.

An unfulfilled relational need can become a button. It's like the verse in James 4:1, "What causes fights and quarrels among you? Don't they come from your desires that battle within you?" We all have things we want to happen that help us feel loved and cared for. Gary Chapman wrote a bestselling book called *The Five Love Languages* that highlights several of these important relational needs: quality time together, words of affirmation, receiving gifts, acts of service, and physical touch. When these love languages (or other relational needs) are left unsatisfied, that triggers something deep within our heart and we react in an effort to get them satisfied.

A button can represent an old hurt. Every time we get emotionally wounded, our brain stores the pain of that experience, and it becomes an area of sensitivity. If something in the present reminds us of the past hurtful experience, it becomes an emotional sore spot or area of extreme sensitivity.

Weakness on both sides is the motto of all quarrels.

—VOLTAIRE

The places where we feel vulnerable, weak, or easily threatened can signify a button. It's easy to feel insecure about trying something new, moving outside your comfort zone, not feeling competent, or even showing emotion.

Some people use the phrase "hot button" to describe a controversial subject or issue that is likely to arouse strong emotions and reactions. Issues like abortion, same-sex marriage, war, gun control, capital punishment, and embryonic stem cell research are all examples of highly charged and sensitive issues that can get us riled up.

Thus, our buttons encompass sensitive issues such as pet peeves, personality discord, fear, unmet expectations, unfulfilled relational needs, past hurts, hot topics, and uncertainty. What gets triggered when our buttons are pushed, however, is a deeper emotion. I'm not talking about basic feelings, like mad, depressed, annoyed, worried, upset, sad, jealous, bored, or tired. Instead, buttons are intense emotions that often come out of our conscious awareness—for example, feeling . . .

- Unloved
- Disrespected
- Rejected
- Failed
- Controlled
- Abandoned
- Inadequate
- Worthless
- Not good enough
- Invalidated
- Unimportant

When we get hurt, frustrated, or argue, it's because our emotional buttons got pushed or triggered. It's important to understand that our day-to-day squabbles over money, chores, kids, and so on are not about the real issues. A real issue is rarely the topic itself; our sensitive emotions got stirred up. This is what's so misleading about an argument. We get so focused on the topic that we miss the root cause. For example, according to research, the top seven issues that married couples argue about are:

1. Money
2. Household chores
3. Children
4. Sex
5. Work
6. Leisure time
7. In-laws[5]

The poolside argument about who should watch the children fits this research finding perfectly—we were number three. Hurray for us! However, all of these topics are surface issues and are never the root of the problem. Observe the emotional roots of these common disagreements that we experience as couples:

- Arguments about *money* can push buttons like feeling insecure or controlled.
- Arguments about *household chores* might push buttons like feeling taken advantage of and misunderstood.
- Arguments about *children* may push buttons like feeling invalidated and helpless.
- Arguments about *sex* can push buttons like feeling rejected or inadequate.
- Arguments about *work* can push buttons like feeling unimportant and misportrayed.
- Arguments about *leisure time* and activities can push buttons like feeling disconnected and misjudged.
- Arguments about dealing with *in-laws* might push buttons like feeling not good enough or disrespected.

Many couples feel stuck in the midst of their conflict, and here's why: They aren't focused on the real issue—they're being sidetracked by the argument topic. It's like the expression "rearranging deck chairs on the *Titanic*." Just like tidying up the deck of a sinking ship is a waste of time, arguing and debating a conflict topic is a waste of time until you deal with the underlying emotional issues. You can't *only* focus on your deep emotions; the topic still has merit. For example, if the issue for you is money (perhaps it's about paying off debt), you need to discuss that topic, but you shouldn't discuss it first. I'll not only show you how to identify your buttons later in this chapter, I'll also show you what to do the next time your buttons get pushed. Then I'll explain how to discuss it healthfully with your spouse and, finally, how to resolve the issue if a solution is needed.

But the buttons that have been pushed need your full attention first because they can have the same effect on your relationship that hitting a massive iceberg had on the *Titanic*. Don't allow the Reactive Cycle to disrupt or destroy your marriage.

HOW TO IDENTIFY BUTTONS

Let's return to the Corpus Christi pool and talk about which buttons got pushed that day. When Erin asked if I would go watch the kids because she didn't feel they were safe, it pushed my "unfair" button, because I thought, *You are the one who doesn't feel safe with my nephew watching our kids. That's your issue. It's unfair for you to interrupt my conversation with my brother and ask me to get them out of the pool. You could have told them to get out or brought them with you.* At the same time, I felt controlled. I was thinking, *It seems like you want me to be responsible for how you feel, and you want me to alleviate your fear for you.* However, the biggest button I have is feeling as though I've failed. I hate feeling like a failure—like I've made a mistake or messed up. After our heated interaction, I thought, *Erin is upset with me; therefore, it proves once again that I'm a failure as a husband.*

Of course, I wasn't aware of these thoughts at the time. During seminars, after hearing me tell this story, women have come running up to me during a break to defend my wife. "She'd been with the kids, and she was hungry!" or "Erin needed a break. How selfish of you to say no when all she wanted was food!" Feelings are neither right nor wrong, good nor bad, logical nor illogical. They are just feelings. By definition, feelings are not logical, but they are a great source of information. And when my buttons got pushed, unfortunately, I wasn't thinking about Erin—I was focused on how to get rid of the unwanted feelings that had flared up. This is why I love the Vincent van Gogh quote, "Don't forget that the little emotions are the great captains of our lives and that we obey them without knowing it." Isn't that a perfect description of how our emotional buttons can seize control of our behavior? If I could have thought all this through, I'm sure I would have done many things differently. But buttons don't work that way. A mind has a difficult time convincing a heart of anything. We can't simply think our buttons away.

What's interesting about Erin and me is that both of us hate to make mistakes. Whereas I go to a place of feeling failed after the mistake, Erin feels worthless. She believes the mistake is evidence of her worthlessness or that people will view her as having no value. Erin also hates it when she feels someone is misjudging her or portraying her in an inaccurate way. Her fear is if she is misportrayed, then people will not see her value. She also feels devalued or worthless when she feels ignored or invisible. Another big button for Erin is feeling invalidated. She wants people to care about and value her feelings, thoughts, and opinions.

It's important to remember that our buttons don't typically follow a logical path. If they did, they'd rarely get triggered. At this point, I'm not focusing on what we could do differently to keep buttons from getting pushed or how we could manage a conflict better. I want to keep the focus on buttons and the fact that we all get them triggered.

You've seen our buttons that were pushed that day, and you might have related to one or more of them. But there are many more emotional buttons. Let's take a look at yours.

IDENTIFYING YOUR BUTTONS

Are you ready to discover your own buttons? Over the years, I've developed a short quiz to help people identify their emotional buttons. As you take the quiz, pay special attention to the key issue: "How did you feel about yourself in the middle of this conflict?" This question is not merely "How did you feel?" (i.e., hurt, frustrated, angry, etc.). Rather, the important point is "When you felt hurt or frustrated, what is the deeper emotion—how did it make you feel about yourself?" This focus will help you pinpoint your buttons.

1. Think about a recent conflict—a negative or hurtful situation with your spouse—something that left you feeling frustrated, hurt, or upset.

2. How did what happened during the conflict make you feel about yourself? You will notice that on the left side of the column is the name of the button, and on the right side is how that button might be defined or what its emotional message says about the individual or the relationship. As you read the list, notice if any of the words or phrases resonate with you. Check all that apply, but star the most important buttons.

"As a result of the conflict, I felt . . ."	What That Feeling Sounds Like
REJECTED	I will be discarded, tossed aside, or replaced.
FAILED	I am not successful; I will not succeed or thrive; I've made a mistake; I haven't performed correctly.
UNWANTED	My spouse doesn't want me or doesn't desire intimacy with me. My spouse is staying in the marriage out of duty, obligation, or because it's the "right" thing to do.
CRITICIZED	My spouse doesn't approve of me. I'm constantly being negatively assessed, analyzed, or critiqued; I feel my spouse's disapproval or condemnation.
ABANDONED	I will be deserted and end up alone. My spouse will ultimately leave me; my spouse isn't committed to me for life.
EXCLUDED	I feel left out of activities, information, or decisions; I feel shut out emotionally from my spouse or that he/she has disengaged.
DISCONNECTED	We are emotionally detached or separated. There are walls or barriers between us in the marriage.
HELPLESS OR POWERLESS	I am weak; I am seen as dependent. I cannot do anything to change my spouse or my situation; I do not possess the power, resources, capacity, or ability to get what I want.
CONTROLLED	I am controlled by my spouse; he/she exercises authority over me. I am made to "submit"; my spouse restrains me. I am treated like a child, or my spouse acts like my parent.
DEFECTIVE	I am flawed or faulty in some way. Something is seriously wrong with me. I'm the problem; I am unlovable.
INADEQUATE	I am not capable; I am incompetent; I am ineffective.
STAGNANT	Our relationship is fruitless, not growing, or stale. Our marriage feels inactive, stationary, or dormant.
INFERIOR	I'm lesser or second-rate. Everyone else is better than I am; I am less valuable or important than others.
INVALIDATED	Who I am, what I think, what I do, or how I feel is not valued by my spouse. My spouse tries to suppress or stifle how I feel.
UNLOVED	My spouse doesn't love me anymore. My spouse feels contempt toward me; my spouse detests or despises me. My relationship lacks warm attachment, admiration, enthusiasm, or devotion.

DISSATISFIED	I do not experience satisfaction within my relationship. I will exist in misery for the rest of my life; I feel no joy in the relationship.
TAKEN ADVANTAGE OF	I will be cheated by my spouse. My spouse takes advantage of me; he/she withholds things I need. I feel like a doormat.
WORTHLESS OR DEVALUED	I have little or no value to my spouse. My spouse fails to recognize my value and worth; I feel cheapened, less than, or undervalued in the marriage. My spouse does not see me as a priceless treasure.
NOT GOOD ENOUGH/DON'T MEASURE UP	Nothing I do is ever acceptable, satisfactory, or sufficient for my spouse. I don't make the grade. I am never able to meet my spouse's expectations of me. My efforts are never enough.
UNACCEPTED	My spouse does not accept me; he/she is not pleased with me. My spouse does not approve of me.
MISJUDGED	I am always being unfairly judged. My spouse forms faulty or negative opinions or beliefs about me. My spouse draws the wrong conclusion about me.
HUMILIATED	I am embarrassed, disgraced, or shamed by my spouse. This marriage is extremely destructive to my self-respect or dignity.
IGNORED/INVISIBLE	I am unnoticed, overlooked, or disregarded. My spouse does not pay attention to me; I feel neglected.
NEGLECTED	I am uncared for or mistreated.
UNIMPORTANT	I am not important to my spouse. I am irrelevant, insignificant, or of little priority to my spouse.
USELESS	I am of no use in my marriage. I am ineffective; I am not needed; I am not necessary in this relationship.
FEAR OF INTIMACY	I am afraid of opening up emotionally. I will be hurt emotionally if I allow my spouse past my "walls."
MISUNDERSTOOD	My spouse does not understand me correctly. He/she has the wrong idea or impression about me. I am misinterpreted or misread.
MISPORTRAYED	My spouse inaccurately portrays me. I am misrepresented or represented in a false way. I am described in a negative or untrue manner. My spouse paints an inaccurate picture of me.
DISRESPECTED	I am insulted. My spouse does not admire me. My spouse has a low opinion of me. My spouse does not respect me; he/she does not look up to me.

OUT OF CONTROL	My marriage is wild, unruly, or hectic. My spouse is unmanageable or uncontrollable. Things feel disorganized or in disarray.
ALONE	I will be by myself or on my own. I will be without help or assistance. I will be lonely; I will be isolated.
INSIGNIFICANT	I am irrelevant to my spouse. I am of no consequence to my spouse. I am immaterial, not worth mentioning, trivial in the eyes of my spouse. I am of minor importance to my spouse.
UNKNOWN	My spouse does not know me. It's like I'm a stranger to my spouse. I am nameless or anonymous to my spouse. I am unfamiliar to my spouse.
BORING	There is no passion in our marriage. My spouse perceives me as dull and dreary. Our marriage is uninteresting. My spouse believes that he/she knows everything there is to know about me. I feel as if we are just roommates—there are no romantic feelings between us.
DISAPPOINTMENT	I will be a letdown in the marriage. My spouse is disappointed in me. My spouse is disillusioned by me.
PHONY	My spouse sees me as fake or not genuine. My spouse believes that I'm a fraud, pretender, or an imposter. My spouse perceives that I'm not who I say I am; I am viewed as a hypocrite.
TREATED UNFAIRLY	My spouse treats me unfairly. My spouse wants me to do things he/she is unwilling to do (there is a double standard). I am asked to do things that are unreasonable or excessive. My spouse treats me differently than others; I am not treated equally.
DECEIVED	Our relationship lacks truth, honesty, or trustworthiness. My spouse willfully perverts truth in order to deceive, cheat, or defraud me. My spouse misleads me or gives a false appearance.
BETRAYED	My spouse is disloyal or unfaithful. My spouse has given up on the relationship. I'll be let down; my spouse will share or reveal private information with others.
UNAWARE	I do not know what is going on in the relationship. I do not have the necessary information. I'm in the dark; I'm clueless. Things feel secretive, hidden, or undisclosed. I'll appear ignorant or uniformed.
UNDESIRABLE	My spouse has no affection or desire for me. I feel unattractive to my spouse. My spouse is bored with me.
OTHER	

Every instance of unproductive or unhealthy conflict you will ever experience happens because of the Reactive Cycle. It's not about money, chores, children, sex, work, time together, or in-laws—these things are the surface issue or topic. The real cause of an argument is that our sensitive areas, vulnerabilities, fears, and deep-seated issues are exposed. And once our deeper emotions have been triggered, we tend to react in negative ways because we aren't always equipped to acknowledge those deep emotions. Often we're not even aware that they exist. Unfortunately, the Reactive Cycle only ends up hurting our relationship and keeps us stuck.

So how do we manage our emotional sensitivities? You've taken a great first step to identify and name your own buttons, but now you must come to terms with what they stem from. Sadly, the buttons that trigger the Reactive Cycle in our marriage originate from lies that have been written on our heart. Debunking those lies is the next step in escaping the Reactive Cycle.

Three

Lies Written on Your Heart

"Pay no attention to the man behind the curtain." This famous line was spoken for the first time when the film version of *The Wizard of Oz* was released throughout the United States in 1939. It was spoken by the character Oscar Zoroaster Phadrig Isaac Norman Henkel Emmannuel Ambroise Diggs (I'm not making this up), a con man who pretends to be "The Great and Powerful Wizard of Oz." However, his scam is exposed when Dorothy's little dog Toto pulls back the giant curtains and reveals the frail old man who has been working the controls for the Wizard of Oz's big fiery face and thunderous voice.

The old man makes a final attempt to bluff Dorothy and her friends—the Scarecrow, the Tin Man, and the Cowardly Lion. "Pay no attention to the man behind the curtain," he protests. "The Great Oz has spoken!" The charade is up as they realize there is no big, scary Wizard but only a small, frail old man. Enraged, Dorothy and team move in to confront the Wizard. "You humbug!" yells the Scarecrow. Dorothy adds her two cents: "You're a very bad man!" All these years later, I still love the Wizard's response to Dorothy's scorn. "Oh, no, my dear," he gently explains, "I'm a very good man. I'm just a very bad Wizard."

There are so many fragile things, after all. People break so easily, and so do hearts.

—NEIL GAIMAN

In terms of the Reactive Cycle, you and I are not bad people; we're just really bad Wizards. On one hand, we use our reactions to deal with the buttons that have been pushed. Unfortunately, this strategy doesn't work, and our negative reactions end up making things worse. However, our reactions do serve a purpose—a hidden purpose. Reactions are like the Wizard's fiery face and thunderous voice in that they act as a distraction or diversion. It's hard for people to see past anger, defensiveness, or withdrawal, so these reactions end up hiding a terrible secret. They mask something that we don't want exposed. Behind the curtain, like the frail and deceptive old Wizard, we conceal painful lies.

THE LIES BEGIN EARLY IN LIFE

When my daughter Taylor was five, we moved into a new neighborhood. We soon discovered that the family next door had recently gone through a difficult divorce. The father had abandoned his family, so the mother was trying to raise four young children alone. As a result, Erin and I encouraged Taylor to befriend Sarah (not her real name), who was also five. We hoped that being around our house would provide Sarah some comfort from the loss of her father and the pain of divorce.

One day Taylor and Sarah were playing in Taylor's room upstairs while I was watching a football game in the family room. Erin had gone shopping.

All of a sudden, a loud argument broke out. I could hear one girl yelling "Yes, they will!" and the other screaming "No, they won't!" Over and over. I imagined that the girls were fighting about Barbie dolls or whatever five-year-olds fight about. I couldn't have been more wrong.

The conflict spilled out into the hall, down the stairs, and came to rest next to my chair. Not wanting to miss any of the game, I quickly asked, "Girls, what's the problem?"

Taylor responded, "Daddy, will you tell Sarah that you and Mommy are not going to get a divorce?"

That pretty much squashed my theory about Barbie.

Realizing that I had encountered a "teachable moment," I muted the TV.

"Sarah," I gently said, "I don't want to take sides, but I'm not going to divorce Taylor's mom and leave."

Taylor instantly celebrated her victory by sticking out her tongue and unleashing the wettest raspberry you've ever seen or heard. She then dashed back up to her room.

As I unmuted the TV, I encouraged Sarah to join Taylor in her room.

Sarah started to leave, took about three steps, and stopped. It seemed like she wanted to say something.

"Is everything okay?" I asked. "Do you need something?"

With a bowed head and a voice barely above a whisper, she said, "Well . . . I was just thinking. Would it be okay if I came back sometime and watched a football game with you? I could pretend that you're my daddy. He left, and I know it's my fault."

I choked back tears as I reassured her that I'd be lucky to have her as my football buddy. I tried to explain why her dad had left and that it had nothing to do with her. But I've come to realize that your brain has a hard time convincing your heart of anything. In the depth of her heart, Sarah believed that her daddy was gone because of her. I'm convinced that the word "rejected" or "abandoned" or "defective" or "unlovable" has been etched with a flint tool on the tablet of her heart.

Sarah's heart is wounded. She is not alone when it comes to messages being written on the heart. We all have wounds that, sadly, begin early in life. The negative experiences we encounter often create emotional injuries. When we go through painful or traumatic events, they frequently define who we are on a heart level. Sadly, when this happens, the result is profound. Our heart wounds ultimately affect our life and shape the way we relate to others—especially our spouse. Let me explain.

God designed us to live life open and connected—"I have come that they may have life, and have it to the full"—but the enemy wants the opposite—"The thief comes only to steal and kill and destroy" (John 10:10). What do you think the evil one is trying to "steal, kill and destroy"? Your heart! So our heart is attacked. One Christian author, in the excellent book *Waking the Dead,* makes a powerful observation:

I find it almost hard to believe a case must be made that the heart is . . . well, at the heart of it all. Of life. Of each person.

Of God. And of Christianity. It is diabolical, despicable, and is downright evil. This bears the mark of the enemy. The enemy knows how vital the heart is, even if we do not, and all his forces are fixed upon its destruction. For if he can disable or deaden your heart, then he has effectively foiled the plan of God, which was to create a world where love reigns. By taking out your heart, the Enemy takes out you, and you are essential to the Story. Once you begin to see with the eyes of your heart, once you have begun to know it is true from the bottom of your heart, it will change everything. The story of your life is the story of the long and brutal assault on your heart by the one who knows what you and your marriage could be and fears it.[1]

I wholeheartedly agree that our life is the story of a long, brutal assault on our hearts. The enemy will use any person (i.e., a parent, family member, friend, classmate, teacher, coach, boss, etc.) or experience (i.e., school, sports, divorce, fitness test, dating, job, home environment, etc.) to severely wound us.

God made it clear that we get both positive and negative messages written on our hearts; "Keep my commands and you will live; guard my teachings as the apple of your eye. Bind them on your fingers; write them on the tablet of your heart" (Proverbs 7:2–3). and "Judah's sin is engraved with an iron tool, inscribed with a flint point, on the tablets of their hearts" (Jeremiah 17:1). Hopefully, you and I received many positive messages that have been etched deeply into our hearts as well, but I know that on this side of heaven, life events work to create painful hurts, wounds, lies, and messages that try to define who we are.

~~~~~~~~~~~~~~~~~

Other people's opinion of you does not have to become your reality.

—LES BROWN

~~~~~~~~~~~~~~~~~

Why does Satan assault our heart? King Solomon, the wisest man who ever lived, gave the answer more than five thousand years ago when he wrote, "Above all else, guard your heart, for it is the wellspring of life" (Proverbs 4:23). Solomon and Satan both understood that our heart is the wellspring of life—the very center of who we are. Literally, what happens to our heart impacts every other dimension of our lives. "For as he thinks in his heart, so is he" (Proverbs 23:7; NKJV). Moreover, what we believe deeply in our hearts becomes our reality. Here's how Shad Helmstetter explains this process:

> Year after year, word after word, our life scripts are etched. Layer by layer, nearly imperceptibly, our self-images are created and in time we join in. We help out. I can't do that. I have never been good at that. I always mess that up. So, we add our two cents to the already big problem. We believe what we are being told by others and what we are telling ourselves. Repetition is a convincing argument. In time we became what we most believed about ourselves.[2]

Do you see how the real battle in this world is over control of our heart? Two Christian authors, in their excellent book *Love & War*, talk about this battlefront:

The great and terrible clash between the Kingdom of God and the kingdom of darkness continues. They are fighting for the human heart. At its core this ancient struggle comes down to one question: Can a kingdom of love prevail? God insists that "love never fails" (1 Corinthians 13:8). Satan laughs. The world laughs.[3]

God's desire is that our hearts be abundantly filled with his truth. This is exactly why we find so many verses in the Bible that talk about abundance:

May the Lord make your love increase and overflow for each other and for everyone else, just as ours does for you. May he strengthen your hearts. (1 Thessalonians 3:12)

I pray that out of his glorious riches he may strengthen you with power through his Spirit in your inner being . . . that you may be filled to the measure of all the fullness of God. (Ephesians 3:16–20)

From this place of abundance, God's desire is that our heart will be open and full of God's love. However, the enemy wants our heart littered with wounds, negative messages, and lies, because they have widespread ramifications for our life and relationships.

HOW THE LIES AFFECT OUR MARRIAGE

A wife was complaining to her friend that her husband gets "historical" when they argue. "You mean hysterical," her friend corrected. "No," the wife said. "Historical. Every time we have an argument, he brings up things that have happened in the last thirty years!" I truly believe that we all get "historical" when we argue. Here is what I mean. I am convinced that the lies, negative messages, and wounds on our heart (our "history") become the basis for most of our emotional buttons that keep us stuck in the Reactive Cycle. Visually, if we could pop the back off a button and look inside, we would find it littered with lies.

So much happens every day within a marriage. Think about the endless combination of words we say, unspoken messages we send, actions we do or don't take, choices we make, and so on. Combine this mixture of words, messages, and behaviors with the lies already written on our heart, and the effects can be explosive. Remember, once a lie is written on our heart, those lies become our deepest beliefs. The problem is that we don't want those beliefs (lies) to be true. We don't want to feel unimportant, unloved, defective, rejected, controlled, or inadequate. So we react. Can you see how some of the lies that you've bought into your marriage and other relationships act like huge buttons that get pushed and cause you to go into reaction mode?

To open your heart to someone means exposing the scars of the past.

—UNKNOWN AUTHOR

Every argument that a husband and wife engages in has its roots in the lies written on their heart. Here is a painful example that happened to some friends of mine who were married less than two years at the time.

Stacy loved Precious Moments figurines. She had been collecting them for many years. Her husband, Carey, had quickly learned that this was a foolproof gift for any special occasion. Carey had even given Stacy an antique glass cabinet so she could proudly display her growing collection.

One day Carey went into a Hallmark store in search of the perfect card for their upcoming anniversary. As he rounded a corner, he noticed a Precious Moments display featuring a special offer. "A Precious Moments of the year club?" Carey thought. "Could I get any luckier?"

Sure enough, if he signed up Stacy, she'd get not only a limited-edition, personalized figurine each year, she would also get a newsletter and other cool stuff that he knew she'd love.

It was going to be one great anniversary!

Carey quickly filled out the complicated paperwork and handed it to the salesclerk.

On their anniversary, Carey proudly handed Stacy her card and special gift. He couldn't wait to see the look of surprise and pure joy on her face.

As Stacy unwrapped the box and examined the figurine, newsletter, and several other items, Carey noticed surprise on her face, but not the kind he'd expected.

"Is everything okay?" Carey inquired.

"I'm just wondering why the figurine is personalized with your name," Stacy said, confused. "Actually, everything says Carey on it. Why?"

"They obviously made a mistake," Carey quickly defended himself. "You're missing the bigger picture. I got you a Precious Moments of the year club. I'll get them to fix the name later. Why are you upset by their stupid error?"

"How could you not use my name?" Stacy reacted. "Obviously, you weren't thinking of me!"

"I did this for you!" Carey shouted, and then walked away.

You might be thinking, "Why did Stacy react that way? It was an obvious mistake." But don't ignore what was really going on in the deep places of her heart. Again, if you try to analyze the Reactive Cycle using your brain, buttons and reactions make no logical sense. You can't use logic or reason to examine matters of the heart. When our buttons get pushed, there is little logical reasoning. But if we peeled back the layers of Stacy's heart, we'd see several lies deeply etched. As a young girl, Stacy grew up constantly feeling unimportant and marginalized. Her parents always seemed too busy to notice her or to pay attention to the little things. Satan was ultimately able to convince her that she didn't matter and wrote on her heart that she was worthless.

The mind forgets, but the heart always remembers.

—ANONYMOUS

Stacy knows that her reaction to Carey was ridiculous. "But in that moment," she explained, "when I saw his name on everything, it was just another example of someone not taking the time to do it right because I'm not worth the effort."

The wounds and messages we receive early in life follow us whether we want them to or not.

The real danger is that these lies on our heart create sensitive areas (buttons) that get pushed and that propel us into the Reactive Cycle. The longer we stay stuck in this dead-end cycle, the more our heart is at risk for shutting down. If we don't deal with our wounds and replace the lies with God's truth, we miss out on a wholehearted marriage, in which love flows freely between two open hearts. We must unshackle our heart so it is fully open and freely able to love. This is why we were encouraged to "Love each other deeply from the heart" (1 Peter 1:22). But we can't do this as long as these lies run rampant throughout our relationships. It's time to fight back!

HEALING THE WOUNDED HEART

We all long for a great marriage, right? Why else would you be reading this book? To get what we want, we must realize that a thriving marriage is possible only when a husband and wife are wholeheartedly engaged. When your heart is fully open, it allows love (along with peace, patience, kindness, and goodness) to flow freely between you and your spouse. As we have seen, the bad news is that Satan wants to prevent our hearts from existing in this state of openness. We end up being wounded by people and life events. It's our responsibility to nurse these wounds back to health so we can engage wholeheartedly with our loved ones. I've found that healing a wounded heart is a three-step process.

Step 1:
Identify the Lies on Your Heart

First and foremost, we need to identify the lies that have been written on our heart. It's impossible to escape this fallen world unscathed. Sadly, no one is impervious to Satan's power to influence us with lies and negative messages. None of us had a perfect family or perfect childhood. Everyone has been wounded in some way.

Identifying lies on your heart doesn't mean that you're blaming everything on your past. I'm not suggesting that you make others responsible for the hurtful events you've experienced. And yet it's important to understand how the past might be influencing your current situation. The good news is that God wants to help, so you don't have to do this by yourself. In Psalms 139:23, David prays, "Search me, God, and know my heart; test me and know my anxious thoughts." He is asking God to search his heart and help him identify the messages that have been written there. You can ask God to search *your* heart for lies and messages; you can pray for God to show you what is written on your heart. God wants to reveal the answer if you are willing to seek out the information. "You will seek me and find me when you seek me with all your heart" (Jeremiah 29:13).

Your heavenly Father mourns the lies and messages that the evil one has falsely inscribed on your heart. Your heart is the place He most wants to heal. "He has sent me to bind up the brokenhearted, to proclaim freedom for the captives" (Isaiah 61:1). Your imprisoned heart is the exact place He wants to pour His love. Be like King David, "a man after God's own heart," and ask God what is written on your heart. He knows what the walls of your heart look like. Pray that God will open the eyes of your heart. "I pray that the eyes of your heart may be enlightened" (Ephecians 1:18). As you pray, focus on the painful experiences from your past that you can remember (disappointments, setbacks, failures, times you were hurt, traumatic events, etc.). Now consider how an event made you feel about yourself. What did you say to yourself? What conclusions did you draw about yourself? What were the messages that you received from the incident?

The heart has eyes which the brain knows nothing of.

—CHARLES H. PERKHURST

If you can't remember any specific experiences from your childhood, you may gain insight from a recent conflict with your spouse. How did the argument make you feel about yourself? What were the messages it communicated about you?

Think about a recent conflict with your spouse or another significant loved one (parents, kids, siblings, extended family, etc.). You might first be aware of feeling frustrated, hurt, mad, upset, or angry. But try to find the deeper emotion—worthless, betrayed, rejected, unloved, disrespected, not good enough, abandoned. Now go deeper still. What did the negative interaction say about you? What did the hurtful message communicate about who you are deep inside?

To help, below are some of the most common buttons and the corresponding lie or message that gets written on the heart.

My Button	The Lie Written on My Heart
REJECTED	My spouse doesn't want me.
ABANDONED	I will be deserted and end up alone.
DISCONNECTED	We will become emotionally detached or separated.
FAILED	I will not perform correctly; I am not good enough.
HELPLESS	I cannot do anything to change my spouse or my situation.
INADEQUATE	I am incompetent. Everyone else is better than I am.
INVALIDATED	Who I am, what I think, what I do, or how I feel is not valued.

UNLOVED	My spouse doesn't love me anymore.
NOT GOOD ENOUGH	I don't measure up; I am never able to meet my spouse's expectations.
WORTHLESS	I am useless; I have no value.
UNIMPORTANT	I am irrelevant, insignificant, or of little priority to my spouse.
DISRESPECTED	My spouse does not show me the respect I deserve.
DEFECTIVE	I am flawed; there is something wrong with me; I'm the problem.
CONTROLLED	My spouse wants to be the boss of me.

Your job is to become aware of the messages etched on your heart. By the way, it's okay if there are multiple lies written on your heart or feelings that are not on this list. All that matters is that you identify the lies and messages that are written there.

Our hearts are amazingly valuable and incredibly vulnerable. While identifying the wounds is a good start, it's not enough. We'll have to dig deeper to replace the lie with the truth. Let's get those messages removed so that you can come to your marital conflicts with a focus on Christ and His truth instead of a reaction based on lies.

Step 2:
Replace the Lie with the Truth

You may be thinking, "I see the messages on my heart, and I get that they are not true. So let's move on." I wish it were that simple. Keep in mind that the lies were "firmly" etched on your heart. "Judah's sin is engraved with an iron tool, inscribed with a flint point, on the tablets of their hearts" (Jeremiah 17:1). Notice that it says "flint point." In other words, the lies have been scratched and cut deeply into your heart. You cannot simply think them away. It's easy to think, I *know* the lie isn't true. But I can guarantee that if there's a battle between your heart and head, your heart will always win. I guess the good and bad news is that your heart is more persuasive than your head. You cannot outwit or rationalize away what is written on your heart. Remember, the Bible makes this point clear through King Solomon: "As a man thinks in his heart so he is" (Proverbs 23:7). It doesn't say "as a man thinks in his head."

As you did to identify the messages, let's look at two key resources available to help you discover the truth about you and your heart.

TRUTH RESOURCE 1:
Our Heavenly Father, Christ, and the Holy Spirit

"My flesh and my heart may fail, but God is the strength of my heart" (Psalm 73:26). Isn't that a wonderful verse? When our heart fails because it's littered with lies, God is our strength. Why? Simply put, He is the ultimate source of truth. When we pray to God, we also get to speak to Jesus and the Holy Spirit, which is fantastic news, because they are called "truth." There are so many verses in the Bible about Jesus being the truth. Here are two of my favorites:

> *Jesus answered, "I am the way and the truth and the life." (John 14:6)*

> *Grace, mercy and peace from God the Father and from Jesus Christ, the Father's Son, will be with us in truth and love. (2 John 1:3)*

Furthermore, when Jesus tells the disciples that He is leaving, He comforts them with the news that He will send a helper. "And I will ask the Father and he will give you another Counselor to be with you forever—the Spirit of Truth" (John 14:16–17). The Bible goes on to say, "And it is the Spirit who testifies, because the Spirit is the

truth" (1 John 5:6). What a great comfort it is to know that the Holy
Spirit's job is to counsel us and remind us about the truth of who
God created us to be: "But when he, the Spirit of truth, comes, he
will guide you into all truth" (John 16:13). This truth is waiting—all
we have to do is ask.

Holley Gerth, author of *You're Already Amazing: Embracing Who
You Are, Becoming All God Created You to Be,* writes about her struggle
with the lies on her heart and the freedom she's discovered through
God's amazing truth. Listen to her words:

I have a confession. I'm intimidated by you. And by you, I
mean women.

Put me in a room of my peers and it won't be long before
my hands are sweaty and I'm shaking in my boots (yeah, the
cute ones I bought from T. J. Maxx in the hopes they'd somehow hypnotize everyone into liking me—you know what I'm
talking about). It got so bad I even took drastic measures a few
summers ago. I went to the library and I checked out all the
social skills books. The ones like, *How to Have Friends and Influence People Without Relying on Your T. J. Maxx Boots.* And I read all
of them. I know—don't say I didn't warn you.

Through my ambitious pursuit of coolness, I discovered
that my insecurities came from a much deeper place than an
inability to make coherent small talk at times. What I thought
might be some sort of social ailment turned out to be a spiritual one.

Inside a voice whispered, "You're not enough." Depending
on the day, an extra word might be thrown into that sentence—

You're not pretty enough.
You're not outgoing enough.
You're not likable enough.

So I kept spinning my wheels on an endless treadmill. I'd make progress in one area only to realize I had miles to go in another.

Exhausted, I finally began pondering and praying. "Lord," I asked, "why do women feel as if we're not enough?" It seemed I heard a whisper in response, "Because they're not." For a moment I thought I had some holy static happening.

"Excuse me, God, it sounded like you said, 'We're not enough.' Could you repeat that, pretty please?" Again, gently and firmly, "You are not enough."

By then I started thinking perhaps my heart had dialed the wrong number and the devil was on the line. But in that pause it seemed God finished the sentence, "You are not enough . . . in me you are so much more."

We are much more than pretty . . . we are wonderfully made.

We are much more than likable . . . we are deeply loved.

We are much more than okay . . . we are daughters of the King.

I think the enemy tricks us into believing we are not enough because he knows if we discover the truth we'll be unstoppable. If you've embraced that lie like I did, then together we can start trading it for the truth. We are chosen, cherished, created sons and daughters of God who have all we need to fulfill His plans for our lives. He has made us just as He wants us to be. We have something to offer that no one else can bring . . . and the world is waiting.[4]

The world is waiting . . . your spouse is waiting . . . your kids are waiting for your healed and open heart. Remember, the story of your life is the story of the long and brutal assault on your heart by the one who knows what you and your marriage could be and fears it.

Jesus said that He came to heal the brokenhearted. "He heals the brokenhearted and binds up their wounds" (Psalm 147:3). Let Him heal your wounded heart by speaking the truth to you. Am I really a failure? Is my wife Erin really worthless? Are you really alone, unlovable, disrespected, inadequate, and so on? Whatever the lie, take it to God so He can cleanse your heart with His truth. He desperately wants your heart decontaminated and fully open. Thus, your job is to block out all of the distractions and other voices and fine-tune the ears of your heart to His voice—that small still voice (1 Kings 19:12). The music group Casting Crowns has a great song called "Voice of Truth" that so perfectly captures this point. Listen to these two lines from their life-changing lyrics:

Out of all the voices calling out to me
I will choose to listen and believe the voice of truth.[5]

Satan uses your mind, past experiences, and people to lie to you. But the Lord, the voice of truth, hungers to speak truth into your broken and wounded heart: "The Spirit of the Sovereign LORD is on me, because the LORD has anointed me to proclaim good news to the poor. He has sent me to bind up the brokenhearted, to proclaim freedom for the captives and release from darkness for the prisoners" (Isaiah 61:1). Will you choose to listen and believe the voice of truth?

TRUTH RESOURCE 2:
The Holy Bible

The Scriptures are overflowing with verse after verse that tell us the truth about the power of God's words. Listen to these great verses.

Trust in the Lord with all your heart, and do not lean on your own understanding. (Proverbs 3:5–6)

Love the Lord your God with all your heart . . . these command-
ments that I give you today are to be upon your hearts. (Deuteronomy
6:5–6)

My son, be attentive to my words; incline your ear to my sayings. Let
them not escape from your sight; keep them within your heart. For they
are life to those who find them, and healing to all their flesh. (Proverbs
4:20–22)

Keep my commands and you will live; guard my teachings as the apple
of your eye. Bind them on your fingers; write them on the tablet of your
heart. (Proverbs 7:2–3)

I will never forget the night God used the amazing truths in His
word to heal a lie forming in my daughter Murphy's heart when she
was thirteen years old. One evening when I returned home from
work, I found Murphy up in her room crying.

"What's wrong, honey?" I gently asked. "Did something happen
at school today?"

"I don't want to talk about it," Murphy said through her tears.

I never quite know if I should honor her silence or if I should
push through it. Fortunately, it was one of those moments when
God intervened and whispered in that small, still voice that I should
just be quiet and hold my precious girl.

As we lay on her bed in silence, Murphy finally said, "Boys are
so stupid!"

I wanted to ask if she had been talking to Mommy again, but I
resisted. "I agree," I joked. "And it only gets worse . . . wait until you
get married."

Murphy's elbow to my rib cage suggested that she wasn't ready to
joke about it.

"What happened today?" I asked again.

"Kaitlyn and I were sitting at the boys' table today at lunch," Murphy explained. "This one boy got mad that we were 'invading' their table. He kept yelling at us to leave."

"And what did you say?"

"You're not the boss of me!"

I've never been more proud of my daughter. She has so much of her mama in her.

"But then he started calling us names," Murphy said. "He told me that I was ugly and that I was worthless. He even said that I would never be able to find a husband."

My sweet girl just sobbed and sobbed. You could tell that his insensitive words were starting to take root deep in her heart. And the evil one was playing sculptor. You could just imagine him with a chisel and hammer, starting to carve away on her young heart.

Not tonight. Not on my watch.

"Why would you let this boy decide what is true about you?" I asked. The sobs continued. "Murphy," I questioned, "what is Satan trying to get you to believe?"

She thought for a moment, then said, "That I'm worthless. That I'm ugly. And that I'll never make a good wife."

"But what is the truth?" I said firmly. "And not what you think or what I think but what God thinks—what does He say in His Word about you?"

It's amazing how we start to calm down when the focus turns to our heavenly Father. "Search me, O God, and know my heart; test me and know my anxious thoughts" (Psalm 139:23). There is a reason why David prayed this prayer. "Be still, and know that I am God" (Psalm 46:10).

My prayer was Ephesians 1:18, that the eyes of my daughter's heart might be enlightened. Murphy and I spent the next thirty minutes searching the Scriptures to find what her Heavenly Father thought about her. In the end, my daughter discovered several powerful verses to neutralize Satan's attack.

Lie #1: *You are ugly.*

The Truth: "The Lord does not look at the things man looks at. Man looks at the outward appearance, but the Lord looks at the heart" (1 Samuel 16:7).

"Dad," explained Murphy, "my heart is beautiful and that is what's most important to God." I also found this great verse: "The King is enthralled by your beauty" (Psalm 45:11). I fought back tears as my daughter's heart recognized the truth—that she is beautiful.

Lie #2: *You are worthless.*

The Truth: "For you are my treasured possession" (Exodus 19:5).

"The God of this universe thinks that I'm his treasured possession," Murphy agreed, "and Jesus considers me his 'glorious inheritance'" (Ephesians 1:18).

Lie #3: *You'll never find a husband.*

The Truth: "The Lord God said, 'It is not good for the man to be alone. I will make a helper suitable for him'" (Genesis 2:18).

"I know that God doesn't want me to be alone," Murphy insisted, "and the Lord says that if I delight in Him, he will give me the desires of my heart [Psalm 37:4]. I want to get married, and I trust that God will bring the perfect 'helpmate' for me someday. I know that I'm valued, and that I'm beautiful, and that I'm going to make a great wife."

Yes! "Then you will know the truth, and the truth will set you free" (John 8:32).

Prayer and Scripture. This is what Paul meant when he said, "Stand firm then, with the belt of truth buckled around your waist" (Ephesians 6:14).

Murphy had been reading the Bible for years, but she did not tap in to the healing power of the Scripture until she got specific with what she was looking for. The key is to find specific verses that speak directly against the lies and messages. Satan has leveled a specific attack against you with explicit lies and messages. Thus, using exact truth as your counterattack is the best way to heal the wounds written on your heart. Therefore, we must memorize these verses, meditate on them, and continuously recite their power. Watch how God's words can challenge the fears and lies in the chart below.

Emotional Button	The Truth Written on My Heart
REJECTED OR ABANDONED	"I will never leave you nor forsake you." (Joshua 1:5); "I have loved you with an everlasting love." (Jeremiah 31:3)
ALONE	". . . And surely I am with you always, to the very end of the age." (Matthew 28:20); "God makes a home for the lonely." (Psalm 68:6, NASB)
COWARDLINESS	"Be on your guard; stand firm in the faith; be men of courage; be strong. Do everything in love." (1 Corinthians 16:13)
UNLOVED	"How great is the love the Father has lavished on us . . ." (1 John 3:1)
FAILURE	"If your descendants watch how they live, and if they walk faithfully before me with all their heart and soul, you will never fail." (1 Kings 2:4)
HELPLESS OR POWERLESS	"He gives strength to the weary and increases the power of the weak . . . but those who hope in the Lord will renew their strength." (Isaiah 40:29–30)

CONTROLLED	"I have been crucified with Christ and I no longer live, but Christ lives in me." (Galatians 2:20)
UNWANTED	"I gave up everything I loved that I might gain your love." (Romans 8:31–32); ". . . and he was called God's friend." (James 2:23)
DEFECTIVE	"You are fearfully and wonderfully made." (Psalm 139:14)
UNKNOWN	"You may not know me, but I know everything about you. I know when you sit down and when you rise up. I am familiar with all your ways." (Psalm 139:1–3)
INTIMACY	"Keep me safe, O God, for in you I take refuge." (Psalm 16:1)
DISCONNECTED	"And nothing will ever separate you from my love." (Romans 8:31–32)

It's all in there. Whatever the lie is, God commands us to "write his word on the tablet of our heart" (Proverbs 7:3) and "hide the word in our hearts" (Psalm 119:11) because the Bible is such an important source of truth.

Are you exhausted yet? Identifying the lies and messages in your heart can be emotionally draining, to say the least. But rejoice! Your marital conflicts do not need to be controlled by the negative messages and lies of the world and Satan. Using God's truth, bask in the certainty that you are valuable, you will never be alone or abandoned, you are strong and successful in Christ, you are unconditionally accepted, and you measure up and are good enough.

Don't forget: "Above all else, guard your heart, for it is the wellspring of life." Your heart is the wellspring of God's love. And when you guard your heart with that beautiful truth, you are in for a wholehearted connection with your spouse like you never knew you could experience.

Now that you understand the first half of the Reactive Cycle—your buttons getting pushed—let's explore your knee-jerk reactions and see if you're a fighter or flighter.

Four

Knee-Jerk Reactions

During a counseling session, my clients Holly and Mike (not their real names) told me a story. One Saturday afternoon, Holly asked Mike to help her clean the house. However, Mike had other ideas. He wanted to wash their vehicles in the driveway with the kids.

"To me, cleaning up the house is way more of a priority than washing our cars," Holly declared.

"I'll help after we are done washing the cars," Mike replied. "Just save me a room or two, and I'll get to it when I'm done with the kids." I'm sure that in hindsight, Mike would agree there might have been a better way to negotiate Holly's request!

Mike and the kids had a blast washing the vehicles. While Holly was inside slaving away with the vacuum, they were outside having a massive water fight that spilled over onto a huge blow-up water slide they had just purchased. Mike was cracking up watching them fly down the Slip 'n Slide and crash over the edge onto the grass.

Meanwhile, their three-year-old daughter, Hannah, was playing next to Mike in her plastic kiddie pool.

Life is 10 percent what happens to you and 90 percent how you react to it.

—CHARLES SWINDOLL

As the big kids were performing death-defying tricks on the slide, Hannah announced that she had to go potty. Not wanting to miss any of the action, Mike simply told her to go tell Mommy, who would help her go to the bathroom. Mike justified sending her to Holly because he didn't want to leave the older kids alone while they were roughhousing on the slide. Plus, he didn't want to stroll through their house with wet, grassy feet, especially since Holly was cleaning.

Mike patted Hannah on the bottom as he told her to go find Mommy.

It wasn't thirty seconds before Hannah showed up with a message from Holly. "Mommy says that *you* need to change me!"

Mike was amazed by how his three-year-old daughter was able to deliver that particular mandate with Holly's exact tone and body language. "Holly," he shouted, "can't you change her real quick? You're already inside."

The back door flew open, and Holly hissed, "Her swimming suit is full of poop! This is why I asked you to put her swim diaper on before you let her wash the car."

"I didn't think she really needed a swim diaper," Mike defended. "Plus, the diaper was in the house, and I was already outside."

Holly didn't even need to use words; her look clearly communicated, "Brilliant plan, genius! It appears like that really worked out well for you!" (She used the same look in therapy while telling the story.) What Holly did say was, "If you had helped me clean, like I'd asked, this wouldn't have happened. You always ignore me!"

"I'm not one of your children," Mike shot back. "You can't tell me to clean on your schedule. I said I would help when I was done washing the cars."

"Explain then why you're just sitting here watching the kids play on the slide," Holly argued. "Is this part of the deluxe car-wash package?"

Needless to say, their "discussion" escalated quickly into a fight about household responsibilities, who worked harder, and who did more, until Mike walked away in stony silence. Mike and Holly ended up disconnected with two hearts that were completely closed. Not the best way to spend a gorgeous Saturday afternoon!

Defensiveness. Criticism. Escalation. Sarcasm. Withdrawal. When our buttons get pushed and we react negatively like Mike and Holly did, sadly, we are capable of doing and saying many relationally harmful things, and none of them help us get what we want or help strengthen our marriage. Our knee-jerk reactions are lousy for promoting intimate connections. So why do we react in such negative ways? Why does it seem like one second you can be feeling happy and carefree, and the next second, something happens that throws you for a loop? The answer actually lies in your brain.

People react to fear, not love—they don't teach that in Sunday school, but it's true.

—RICHARD NIXON

THE AMYGDALA HIJACK

There are two parts of your brain—one that thinks and one that feels. As information enters into the brain from your eyes or ears, it goes simultaneously to the amygdala (the emotional center) and the neocortex (the thinking center) to determine what you should do with the information. The good news is that it's usually your thinking brain that decides how you should respond. However, when your buttons are pushed, your amygdala often hijacks your brain before you can make a good decision, and you end up going into reaction mode (fight or flight). For example, imagine you're on your way to the mall during Christmas season. You've had a particularly bad day, and nothing is going your way. While you circle the rows of parked cars, like a hawk seeking its prey, you spot a woman getting into her car. You race around to that aisle like a rocket that's just been launched. As you're about to turn in to the parking space after waiting for what seems to be hours, someone cuts you off and takes the spot. You slam your palms against the steering wheel and shout some choice words that your toddler is now reprimanding you for saying: "We're not supposed to say 'idiot.'"

You can thank the amygdala for that emotional outburst.

All of your reactions—like when you criticize your spouse, yell at the slow-moving traffic, shout at your child for spilling on the carpet, or send that anger-laced e-mail—happen because your amygdala gets hijacked. Why do our brains work this way?

Knee-jerk reactions typically happen because the amygdala's job is to protect you by comparing incoming new data with existing data. However, since the amygdala is constantly scanning for anything that may hurt us, it can distort things quickly because it processes information 250 times faster than your thinking brain.[1] Any strong emotion, such as hurt, fear, frustration, stress, anxiety, anger, or betrayal, hijacks the amygdala and paralyzes the rational part of your brain. Studies have found that you can be in this state for a total of eighteen minutes.[2] As one author put it, "For this time you are highly illogical, emotional, and basically in 'fight or flight' mode—you are not able to think rationally for these 18 minutes. There's little or no ability to rely on intelligence or reasoning."[3] Notice some famous amygdala hijackings straight from the headlines:

- Mike Tyson biting off part of Evander Holyfield's ear in their 1993 title boxing rematch.
- During the 2006 soccer World Cup finals, in front of 28.8 billion viewers in 213 countries, the captain of the French national team, Zinedine Zidane, head-butted Italian player Marco Materazzi and was ejected. The French team ultimately lost the game.
- Joe Wilson (U.S. politician) shouting "You lie!" to President Barack Obama during the president's speech to the joint session of Congress in September 2009.
- Serena Williams's abusive language toward a lineswoman during a match against Kim Clijsters in 2009.
- Kanye West's interruption of Taylor Swift's acceptance speech during the 2009 MTV Video Music Awards.[4]

The amygdala is useful when we are in danger, during times of severe stress, or under enormous pressure. But the amygdala is not great for logic and reason. It's as if you're operating on sheer emotion and are unable to think straight. It's like losing ten to fifteen IQ points temporarily, which explains the "What was I thinking?" phenomenon when you react.[5] When the hijack passes, you still have the fight-or-flight hormones and adrenaline racing through your body for another three to four hours, during which time you'll be rather defensive, sensitive, and prone to emotional reactions.[6] These feelings can linger, keeping you in a negative frame of mind for a good part of the day. Once the thinking brain is in control again, we usually end up feeling guilty and regretting what we we've said and done in reaction mode.

The moment we want to believe something, we suddenly see all the arguments for it, and become blind to the arguments against it.

—GEORGE BERNARD SHAW

Becoming aware of that simple (actually, rather complex) brain function helps us understand why we react so irrationally sometimes and say or do things that we later regret. Let's further explore the fight-or-flight function of the amygdala hijack and how it relates to the Reactive Cycle.

FIGHT OR FLIGHT

After months of working with one fighting couple, I saw a ray of hope when the wife addressed her husband as "hon."

"See, there's still hope for this marriage if you can call him 'hon,'" I said, encouraged.

"I've been calling him that for years," said the wife. "Attila the Hun."

Just like this wife, most of us consciously or unconsciously fall into well-worn patterns of reacting when someone pushes our buttons. We don't like how it feels when a button is pushed, and we'll do or say anything to soothe the hurt or avoid unwanted feelings, including insulting our partner, like this wife does. Did you know that when our buttons get pushed, every reaction is going to be either a fight or a flight?

Think for a moment about a wild animal that gets cornered or surprised—what does it do? One common response is for it to get ferocious, baring its teeth and growling (think grizzly bear). Another common response is to freeze (think possum) or run away (think deer). God's creatures were created with an ability to react quickly to emergency situations. Scientists call this the fight-or-flight reaction. We are no different. In fact, in times of danger or conflict, the adrenaline surges throughout our body to get us ready to protect ourselves. It's no wonder so many of us feel stirred up emotionally, out of control, or desperate to avoid an argument in the midst of the Reactive Cycle.

Before we talk about how we react when our buttons get pushed, I want to clarify something important. Throughout the book, I use the words "react" and "respond." Many people use these terms interchangeably. As I just explained, God created our amygdala (fight-or-flight center) to help protect us. However, when I talk about the word "react" and how we fight or take flight during conflict, I'm always referencing the negative reactions (i.e., anger, defensiveness, withdrawing, etc.) when our buttons are pushed.

For the sake of clarity, I will never use the word to convey something positive, even though, of course, we can react positively; in the context of this book, to react is always harmful to us as individuals, to our spouse, and to our marriage. On the other hand, I use the word "respond" to mean the opposite of a knee-jerk reaction. When we respond to our spouse, I'm talking about positive behaviors (i.e., kindness, gentleness, self-control, etc.) that build up our spouse and help strengthen our marriage.

So, which *reaction* style do you tend to favor—fight or flight? Certainly, it's not an "either/or"; rather, it's a "both/and." How you react will depend on where you are, which button gets pushed, and who does the pushing. I've noticed that I tend to fight with Erin, but I tend to take flight at the office. Let's talk first about the fighters.

FIGHT

A couple I counseled told me a story about a drive they were on down a country road, during which they didn't say a word to each other. An earlier discussion had led to an argument, and neither of them wanted to concede. As they passed a barnyard of mules, goats, and pigs, the husband asked sarcastically, "Relatives of yours?"

"Yep," the wife replied. "In-laws." (As you can imagine, I had to hold back my laughter during our session!)

Just like this husband and wife, those of us who are fighters tend to go after the other person by directly engaging and fighting it out verbally. We might get angry, criticize, get sarcastic, yell, throw a tantrum, debate their position, make belittling comments, defend ourselves, invalidate feelings, jump into fix-it mode, complain, and so on.

The key trait of a fighter is *engagement*. Fighters stand in close and direct confrontation. They don't back down or remain silent—they go toe-to-toe or pursue their spouses around the house. Fighters are usually more passionate, louder, and more energetic; they don't shy from a lively debate. They resolve issues by getting everything out in the open. It's as if the fighter ends up thinking, "Since we are not going to connect relationally, I might as well win the argument." I'm thinking that strategy doesn't work out really well!

If you judge people, you have no time to love them.

—MOTHER TERESA

A fighter's main goal is to persuade his or her spouse. Fighters jump right into a conflict discussion and advocate for their own opinion, viewpoint, or perspective. Thus, fighters spend the majority of their time in persuasion mode. Their discussions can be littered with "yes, you do" and "no, I don't." The goal seems to be to win or outdo their spouse's complaints rather than to be compassionate. Fighters are more likely to interrupt with questions than to listen patiently. They censor few of their thoughts and can be brutally honest. However, don't confuse a fighter with a boxer or a UFC cage fighter—aggressive, yelling, antagonistic, angry, violent, etc. It might look like that, but fighters may also appear controlled, laid-back, and logical as they argue and debate. Many times over the years, Erin, in a state of exasperation, has yelled, "I want to see some emotion from you!" As a fighter, I don't yell or intimidate; instead, I become stoic and stay reasonably calm, cool, and collected. Even though I don't get really emotional, I'm every bit as engaged as Erin is, committed to proving my point or my innocence. Here are the kinds of reactions fighters might employ in the midst of conflict. See if any of these sound familiar.

- Complain, whine, or grumble
- Criticize—express disapproval by attacking the other person's personality or character with judgment ("You're so irresponsible")
- Invalidate—indirectly or directly question, ridicule, or devalue

your spouse's feelings or thoughts ("That's not how you feel" or "Your feelings are ridiculous")

- Blame ("This is your fault")
- Get defensive—attempt to explain, justify, or rationalize your behavior ("If you'd just let me explain")
- Minimize or marginalize your spouse's feelings or ideas ("It's not that big of a deal")
- Go into fix-it mode—focus on finding a solution or solving the problem
- Pursue the truth—argue about what really happened ("It wasn't two weeks, it was like ten days ago")
- Argue about who is right and who is wrong
- Use humor or laughter to divert attention from the issue
- Belittle—use insulting names, mocking tone of voice, sarcasm, or demeaning language ("You're just like your father")
- Escalate—negative comments that spiral into increasing anger and frustration
- Get angry
- Catastrophize—exaggerate or overstate your case ("you never" or "you always")
- Seize control—manipulate your spouse into doing what you want
- Become dishonest or share half-truths
- Act out (i.e., drugs, alcohol, affairs, etc.)

Someone who chooses to fight and engage his or her spouse in a destructive manner always sends the same message: "You're not safe with me." When we defend ourselves, invalidate, belittle, or escalate the argument, we cause our spouse to feel emotionally unsafe. We also pay a personal price as a fighter. According to medical experts, anger and other extreme negative emotions can hurt more than your marriage—there is a significant link between anger and heart disease.[7]

Whereas fighters will overtly engage their spouse when a button gets pushed, "flighters" do the exact opposite.

FLIGHT

I once heard a story about a man who approached his pastor of twenty-five years after church one Sunday afternoon and asked if they could meet in private.

"Pastor, I've got something to tell you," the man said inside the pastor's office. "I've never told this to a soul. It's extremely difficult to tell you this now, but my wife and I have had a fight every day for the past thirty years of our marriage."

The pastor was shocked and didn't know what to say to the man, who was a respected leader in the church. Playing for time to gather his thoughts, the pastor responded, "Every day?"

"Yes, every day," the man confessed.

"Did you fight today before you came to church?" asked the pastor.

"Yes."

"Well, how did it end up?"

"She came crawling to me on her hands and knees."

"What did she say?"

"'Come out from under that bed, you coward, and fight like a man!'"

The silent killer of marriage is emotional disconnection, as seen in this man. We go into flight mode if we avoid conflict or withdraw when the conversation becomes difficult. That is exactly what the first couple did after they sinned in the garden; it's one of the first examples of a flight reaction that we find: "He answered, 'I heard you in the garden, and I was afraid because I was naked; so I hid'" (Genesis 3:10).

The key trait of flighters is a reluctance to get into a disagreement (avoidance) or to stay with an important conversation (withdrawal).

They don't want to rock the boat, so they fly below the radar or stay out of the fray. Withdrawal can be as obvious as walking out of the room or as subtle as staying put but logging off emotionally. Flighters may withdraw by becoming silent or quickly agreeing to a solution just to end the discussion, with no intention of ever returning to the conversation. It's not that they don't talk or interact with their spouse; instead, they avoid sensitive issues, work hard to minimize conflict, and believe there is little gain from getting upset. Their motto is "relax—problems have a way of working themselves out." In avoidance mode, flighters may use the phrase "agree to disagree" time and time again, which means that they avoid conversations they think will end in conflict. Here are the kinds of reactions a flighter might employ in the midst of conflict:

- Withdraw—leave the conversation, either physically or emotionally ("I'm done with this discussion"). As high as 85 percent of withdrawers are men.
- Avoid—evade the conversation, issue, or your spouse ("I don't see why we need to talk about this right now").
- Disconnect—emotionally detach from your spouse ("I don't want to be around you right now").
- Stonewall—remove yourself from the conversation by turning into a stone wall (silent treatment).
- Isolate—go into seclusion or into your "cave."
- Mind read—make assumptions about your mate's private feelings, behaviors, or motives ("I know exactly what you meant by that remark").
- Withhold—hold back affection, feelings, sexual intimacy, or love from your spouse ("I have a headache!").
- Passive-aggressive behavior—use negative or hurtful behavior that is subtle and disguised by actions that appear to

be normal, at times loving and caring ("I don't know how I could have forgotten to pick up the dry cleaning for your big meeting tomorrow").

- Placate—agree to a suggestion with no real intent to follow through, or say "I'm sorry" just to end the conversation ("Okay, you're right").
- Negatively interpret—have exaggerated thoughts about your spouse or believe your spouse's motives are more negative than is really the case ("You always disrespect me in front of the kids!" or "You will never be able to stick to a budget").
- Become indignant—hold a belief that you deserve to be angry, resentful, or annoyed with your spouse because of what he or she did ("He had no right to make that comment about my mother—how dare he").
- Act like an innocent victim—you see your spouse as the aggressor, and you are being unfairly accused, mistreated, or unappreciated ("I was in a perfectly good mood until you started criticizing me").
- Think distress-maintaining thoughts—simmer, stew, and replay the argument over and over.
- Grow apathetic—become pessimistic, distrustful, cynical, and skeptical as you view your spouse and marriage (a closed heart).

A spouse who goes into flight mode and disengages always sends the same message: "I'm disconnecting from any meaningful interaction with you." When we withdraw or avoid conflict, we merely brush our pain and issues under the rug of our heart. However, the piles eventually grow so large that they start to leak out the sides. Unfortunately, what oozes out of a jam-packed heart is depression, worry, explosive rage, bitterness, apathy, substance abuse, or eating disorders.

A woman's flattery may inflate a man's head a little; but her criticism goes straight to his heart, and contracts it so that it can never again hold quite as much love for her.

—HELEN ROWLAND

Studies show that men tend to take the distancing role (flight) more frequently, while women tend to be the pursuer (fighter) and bring up the issues first.[8] The problem with our fight-or-flight reactions is that they are are a complete waste of time! They just don't work. In other words, our reactions never get us anywhere but spinning around in the Reactive Cycle and eventually disconnected.

A CASCADE OF DISTANCE AND ISOLATION

Let me explain why fight-or-flight reactions are so destructive to your relationship. The real problem is that they steadily erode safety in a marriage, and people stop trying to work through their issues. If you cannot constructively manage your conflict and resolve your problems, your marriage is in trouble. For example, if your spouse constantly escalates arguments, you may conclude that it's better to keep your mouth shut. You never reach resolution. Or if you invalidate your spouse over and over, at some point, she will stop sharing how she feels. Nothing gets worked out. If you use critical words to express your feelings, your spouse will quickly learn to withdraw from the conversation. If your style is to withdraw or avoid conflict, problems aren't dealt with. These fight-or-flight reactions can lead to a growing distance and a lack of hope in the marriage.

One of the startling results of research by marriage expert John Gottman is what he calls the Distance and Isolation Cascade.[9] The process begins when, because of these harmful reactions, spouses don't feel heard and understood. When we are not engaged listeners, productive communication is not possible. As time passes, people don't feel emotionally safe and their hearts close. A natural response to emotional disengagement is that couples begin to work out their relational problems on their own and start doing more and more things separately—leisure time, meals, vacations. They move toward parallel lives. Some people leave a marriage through divorce; others leave a marriage by leading parallel lives. Loneliness sets in. And loneliness often kills a relationship. Here is how Neil Rosenthal described the cascade.

> Conflicts that don't get resolved can eventually kill a relationship, because instead of coping with the problem effectively, a couple can get gridlocked over it—having the same conversation about it over and over again with nothing getting resolved. Because they make no headway, they feel increasingly hurt, frustrated and rejected by each other. Criticism, contempt, defensiveness and stonewalling behaviors become ever more present when they argue, while humor and affection become less so. Both people become all the more entrenched in their positions, and less willing to compromise.
>
> Gradually the couple gets overwhelmed. They then start a

slow process of trying to isolate or enclose this area of conflict, but actually they have started becoming emotionally disengaged from each other. They are on the course toward parallel lives and inevitable loneliness—the death knell of any relationship.[10]

The bottom line is that God created us as relational beings. We long for connection. Feeling alone or isolated goes against our natural craving. A marriage is in grave danger if we can't successfully manage conflict or if people feel isolated and alone.

YOUR REACTIONS

Before you can stop the Reactive Cycle in your life, you need to clearly identify your reactions. To help you do this, I've included a simple chart to help you pinpoint the reactions that you typically employ when your buttons get pushed.

Here we go! When you identified your buttons in Chapter 1, you described a recent argument or negative situation with your spouse. With that conflict in mind, think about the different ways that you react. What do you do when your buttons get pushed? What are your common coping strategies you use to deal with your buttons that get pushed?

Check all that apply, but star your most common reactions.

Keep in mind that each conflict is different, and you will not use all of your unique reactions each time. Consequently, as you read through the following list, be sure to check any of the reactions you use within your marriage—even if you didn't use them during that particular conflict.

Reaction	Explanation
ESCALATE	You raise your voice; your emotions spiral out of control.
WITHDRAW	You leave the conversation, either physically or emotionally.
EARN-IT MODE	You try to do more and more to earn your spouse's love and care.
STONEWALL	You remove yourself from the conversation by turning into a stone wall.
BELITTLE	You call your spouse names, use insults, ridicule, take potshots, or mock him or her.
SHUT DOWN	You emotionally disconnect and close your heart.
ARROGANCE	You position yourself as more mature, smarter, superior, or wiser than your spouse.
PACIFY	You try to soothe or calm your spouse; you try to get your spouse not to feel negative emotions.
BLAME	You work to establish blame or place responsibility on your spouse.
CONTEMPT	You become disrespectful or dishonor your spouse with your words or actions.
NEGATIVE INTERPRETATION	You see your spouse through a negative lens and conclude that his or her motives are more negative than is really the case.
CONTROL	You hold back, restrain, oppress, or dominate your spouse. You talk over or prevent your spouse from having a chance to explain his or her position, opinions, or feelings.
INNOCENT VICTIM	You see your spouse as the aggressor and you as being unfairly accused, mistreated, or unappreciated.
DISHONESTY	You tell a lie or half-truth. You fail to reveal important details or give out false information.
ISOLATE	You go into seclusion or into your "cave."
DEMAND	You try to force your spouse to do something, usually with implied threat of punishment if he or she refuses.
WITHHOLD	You hold back your affection, feelings, sexual intimacy, or love from your spouse.
PROVOKE	You intentionally aggravate, hassle, goad, or irritate your spouse.

DENIAL	You refuse to admit the truth or reality.
EXAGGERATE	You make overstatements or enlarge your words beyond bounds or the truth; you make statements like: "You always" or "You never."
DISTRESS-MAINTAINING THOUGHTS	You replay the argument over and over; you can't stop thinking about the conflict or what your spouse did that frustrated or hurt you.
INVALIDATE	You send a subtle or overt message that your spouse's feelings, thoughts, or opinions are wrong, inaccurate, or unacceptable.
REWRITE HISTORY	You recast your earlier times together in a negative light. Your recall of previous disappointments and slights becomes distorted.
INDEPENDENCE	You do your own thing. You become separate from your spouse in your attitude, behavior, and decision making.
PASSIVE-AGGRESSIVE BEHAVIOR	Negative or hurtful behavior that is subtle and disguised by actions that appear normal and at times loving and caring.
DEFENSIVENESS	You try to defend yourself by providing an explanation. You make excuses for your actions.
CLINGINESS	You need to be in constant or close proximity to your spouse.
AVOIDANCE	You evade the conversation, the issue, or your spouse.
ACT OUT	You engage in negative behaviors like drug or alcohol abuse, extramarital affairs, excessive shopping, or overeating.
FIX-IT MODE	You focus almost exclusively on what is needed to solve or fix the problem.
PESSIMISM	You become negative, distrustful, cynical, and skeptical in your view of your spouse and marriage.
COMPLAIN	You express unhappiness or make accusations.
NEGATIVE BODY LANGUAGE	You give a false smile, shift from side to side, or fold your arms across your chest.
CRITICIZE	You pass judgment, condemn, or point out your spouse's faults. You attack his/her personality or character.

STRIKE OUT	You lash out and become verbally or physically aggressive.
MANIPULATION	You attempt to control, influence, or maneuver your spouse for your own advantage.
ANGER	You display strong feelings of displeasure. You experience uncontrolled emotions, such as rage.
CATASTROPHIZE	You experience dramatic, overstated, or exaggerated words or thoughts.
INDIFFERENCE	You become unresponsive to your spouse, you lack interest, sympathy, or concern.
PURSUE THE TRUTH	You try to determine what really happened, who is telling the truth, or whose facts are correct.
ABDICATE	You deny or give away responsibilities.
JUDGE	You negatively evaluate, form an opinion, or conclude something about your spouse.
SELF-DEPRECATE	You run yourself down or become very critical of yourself.
SELFISHNESS	You become more concerned with yourself and your interests, feelings, wants, or desires.
MIND READ	You make assumptions about your spouse's private feelings, behaviors, or motives.
LECTURE	You sermonize, talk down to, scold, or reprimand your spouse.
SELF-ABANDONMENT	You desert or neglect yourself. You take care of everyone except you.
CROSS-COMPLAIN	You meet your spouse's complaint with an immediate complaint of your own, totally ignoring what your spouse has said.
RIGHTEOUS INDIGNATION	You believe that you deserve to be angry, resentful, or annoyed with your spouse because of what he or she did.
WHINE	You express yourself by using a childish, high-pitched nasal tone and stress one syllable toward the end of the sentence.
HUMOR	You use laughter, humor, or joking as a way of not dealing with the issue at hand.
APATHY	You become pessimistic, distrustful, cynical, and skeptical as you view your spouse and marriage.

IGNORE	You stuff down your feelings and thoughts instead of trying to understand or discuss them.
SARCASM	You use negative or hostile humor, hurtful words, cutting remarks, or demeaning statements.
NUMB OUT	You stop feeling and become devoid of emotion.
MINIMIZE	You assert that your spouse is overreacting; you intentionally underestimate, downplay, or soft-pedal the issue or how your spouse feels.
PASSIVITY	You agree to some suggestion with no real intent to follow through, or you say "I'm sorry" just to end the conversation.
RATIONALIZE	You attempt to make your actions seem reasonable. You try to provide believable reasons or credible motives for your behavior.
DUMP ON	You emotionally "vomit," unload, dump, or pile on your spouse.
DISCONNECT	You emotionally detach or disengage from your spouse.
REPEAT YOURSELF	You say your position over and over again, instead of understanding your spouse's position.
RIGHT/WRONG	You argue about who is right and who is wrong; you debate whose opinion, perception, or emotion is the correct one.
STUBBORN	You will not budge from your position. You become inflexible or persistent.
SILENT TREATMENT	You become quiet or "log off" during the conversation.
RIGHTEOUSNESS	You make what you're upset about a moral issue or argue about issues of morality or righteousness.
PLAY DUMB	You pretend not to understand or know what your spouse is talking about.
SULK	You go off and feel sorry for yourself.
SELF-RIGHTEOUSNESS	You become cold and smug because you have such confidence in your righteousness.
NAG	You badger, pester, or harass your spouse to do something you want.

YES, BUT . . .	You start out agreeing (yes), then you end up disagreeing (but).
TANTRUM	You have a sudden outburst of frustration or a fit of temper.
ABUSIVE	You become cruel or violent physically, emotionally, or sexually.
OTHER	

Reactions do not help us reconnect as a couple; create intimacy; or help us effectively manage our conflict. But the real damage is what Satan does to our mind when we're in reaction mode. It's downright diabolical!

Five

Lies About Your Spouse

When you're in the middle of the Reactive Cycle—when your buttons have been pushed and you are in reaction mode (fight or flight)—I believe that Satan immediately goes on the attack. Sharks can detect the presence of blood in the water, even in the smallest amounts, from miles away. Animal experts say that the blood scent is one of the strongest attractants in the animal kingdom.[1] Satan is like those sharks. He is ravenously drawn to blood—especially the emotional kind spilled during unhealthy conflict. And once he detects the blood, he immediately begins circling the injured couple, ready to launch a surprise attack. The problem is, Satan goes after us in a cunning way—he strikes our mind.

The only real power Satan has over Christians is the lies he can get us to believe. Just like Satan writes lies about us on our hearts, he also plants lies about your spouse deep within your subconscious mind. The best chance he has to do this is during the Reactive Cycle, when you're susceptible to spiritual warfare. Could this be why the apostle Paul warned us not to go to sleep while we are still angry? "In your anger do not sin: Do not let the sun go down while you are still angry, and do not give the devil a foothold" (Ephesians 4:25–27).

How does Satan get a foothold in our lives? He attacks us when we are most vulnerable. Paul desperately wanted the early Christians to understand that when we go to bed angry, we are most susceptible to having our mind attacked. However, before I continue, let me give a disclaimer. Spiritual warfare is extremely complex, and I'm not trying to suggest that I know exactly how Satan attacks you as an individual or as a couple. What I'm about to share is only a possibility. And yet, the longer I work with couples, the more I'm convinced that after we take a spin around the Reactive Cycle, Satan immediately launches a full-force attack on our minds, whether we are awake or asleep. I'm confident that our adversary is trying to influence our minds, and there is no better time than when we are shut down, upset, angry, hurt, or emotionally worn out. This is why the apostle Paul wrote: "For our struggle is not against flesh and blood . . . but against the powers of this dark world and against the spiritual forces of evil" (Ephesians 6:12). Just like Satan wants our hearts littered with lies, he also wants our minds filled with deceit about our spouse. However, it's the way that Satan goes about filling our minds with these lies that is downright diabolical—he tries to implant an inception. After all, Satan is "the father of lies."

INCEPTION

In the 2010 blockbuster movie *Inception,* the main character (Leonardo DiCaprio) is hired to perform the act of "inception"— planting an idea within a person's subconscious mind. An idea, positive or negative, is like a virus, because once it's deep in your mind, it grows and impacts you and your relationships, for better or worse. This is exactly what King Solomon understood when he said, "For as he thinks within himself, so he is" (Proverbs 23:7, NAS). Here's a scene from the movie in which DiCaprio's character explains the power of an inception:

What is the most resilient parasite? Bacteria? A virus? An intestinal worm? An idea. An idea is like a parasite—resilient and highly contagious. The smallest seed of an idea can grow. It can grow, define, and destroy you. Once an idea has taken hold of the brain, it's almost impossible to eradicate. An idea that is fully formed—fully understood—now, that sticks, right in there somewhere [pointing to his head]. The subconscious is fueled by emotion, right? Not reason. We need to find a way to translate the inception into an emotional concept. That might work![2]

No offense to Christopher Nolan, the writer and director of *Inception,* but he borrowed this idea from the evil one, who has been using the same strategy for thousands of years. Satan wants to put his wicked, distorted twist on your thoughts about your spouse. He wants to intensify, embellish, amplify, enlarge, magnify, expand—choose whichever verb you like—your negative thinking. Many times in the midst of the Reactive Cycle, I feel like a stage actor who has forgotten his lines: "What's my next line?" The evil one is all too happy to act as director, feeding me line after line. Message after message. Belief after belief. Satan's inception usually comes in the form of an exaggerated message about your spouse based on your original negative interpretation. Satan then takes that single negative interpretation and instantly tries to feed you more lies. With his twisted lines, like a bizarre director, he increases the power of the messages to work you up.

*Every thought is a seed. If you plant crab apples, don't
count on harvesting Golden Delicious.*

—BILL MEYER

Occasionally, I will suggest that my clients keep a diary during
therapy, a way to further understand their conflicts and the way they
engage. Here's one particularly illuminating example. It's easy to see
how our thinking becomes such easy prey for the evil one:

*Her diary: Tonight, I thought my husband was acting weird. We had
made plans to meet at a nice restaurant for dinner. I was shopping with
my friends all day long, so I thought he was upset at the fact that I was
a bit late, but he made no comment on it. Conversation wasn't flowing,
so I suggested that we go somewhere quiet so we could talk. He agreed,
but he didn't say much. I asked him what was wrong; he said, "Nothing." I asked him if it was my fault that he was upset. He said he wasn't
upset, that it had nothing to do with me, and not to worry about it. On
the way home, I told him that I loved him. He smiled slightly and kept
driving. I can't explain his behavior. I don't know why he didn't say, "I
love you, too." When we got home, I felt as if I had lost him completely,
as if he wanted nothing to do with me anymore. He just sat there quietly
and watched TV. He continued to seem distant and absent. Finally, with
silence all around us, I decided to go to bed. About fifteen minutes later, he
came to bed. But I still felt that he was distracted, and his thoughts were
somewhere else. He fell asleep—I cried. I don't know what to do. I'm
almost sure that his thoughts are with someone else. My life is a disaster.*

His diary: Boat wouldn't start, can't figure out why.

Isn't it fascinating how quickly our thoughts can be taken captive and then intensified or exaggerated? Satan wants to infect our marriage by getting us to view our spouse not only in a negative light but in a distorted, exaggerated light. He wants to make us accept as true something far more negative than the truth. Of course, the husband seems to be in flight mode, which is part of the problem. That's exactly where Satan swoops in; he suggests that we take a small problem and make it catastrophic.

When we go through difficult times in our marriage, frequent hurts, frustrations or unmet expectations, disappointments and unhealthy conflict, we often see our spouse in a different way—our perspective changes. As this happens, we switch lenses and start to see our spouse in a negative light. I like how Les and Leslie Parrott explain the impact of negative beliefs:

> Our perception, in how we view a situation, is the result of our attitude. Once we have a particular mind-set, we see everything and everybody in a certain way—either more positively or negatively—even if our perception isn't accurate. That's why in marriage and in life, we so often find what we're looking for. If you think your spouse is lazy, you can find plenty of evidence to support your case. If you think your spouse is efficient, you can find experiences to back that up too. Whatever you have it in your mind to find, you will.[3]

The Greek philosopher Epictetus wrote in the first century: "Men are disturbed not by things, but by the view they take of them." Negative interpretations are destructive because what you think about your spouse—the view you take—you will see and hear even if it isn't true. Paul highlighted this same reality in Romans 14:14: ". . . but to him who thinks anything to be unclean, to him it is unclean." If you believe it's unclean, to you it is unclean. Reality? Truth? These don't matter if you have negative beliefs—those are your reality and truth.

Each of us sees our world through a particular set of senses. If we're not careful, the type of glasses we put on can distort what we're trying to see.

—DEBBIE CHERRY

Aren't these exaggerated, negative beliefs obvious? Why do we believe Satan's lies? I think there are two main reasons we fall prey to his deception so quickly. First, Satan uses our buttons against us in these situations. They are like low-hanging fruit to him. Satan is clever. It says in 2 Corinthians 11:3, "But I am afraid that just as Eve was deceived by the serpent's cunning, your minds may somehow be led astray from your sincere and pure devotion to Christ." Our adversary is cunning and selects the easiest targets with the least amount of effort. Those would be our emotional buttons. It's easy for him to use sensitive emotions to goad us into negative thinking. Satan knows perfectly well that I struggle with feeling like a failure. He understands that I'm very sensitive to thinking that I've made a mistake. So attacking me around this issue is easy pickings, as the expression goes. And he tries to aggravate and intensify our buttons by feeding us distorted lies.

Take my client Julie, for example. She told me one afternoon that she was feeling overwhelmed. There always seemed to be an endless supply of dirty clothes and dishes for this mother of three children. The house was never clean. Julie was trying to keep it all together as she ran kids to athletic practices and piano lessons, tried to get them to school on time and put nutritious meals on the table. There were days when she couldn't seem to get it done. And her husband always seemed to be at the office. She felt alone in her responsibilities of working part-time, managing the household, and caring for their children.

When she was young, Julie's father left her mother for another woman, and Julie had struggled with feeling alone ever since. She took this button into her marriage. Although her husband, John, was a good father and a great provider, Satan, like a lion, moved in for the attack when she was feeling exhausted. To make matters worse, the previous evening, Julie and John fought again about household responsibilities.

"I need help!" yelled Julie.

"I work full-time, plus overtime," John stated defensively.

"And what do you call what I do?" Julie shot back. "Do you think that I'm sitting around all day watching soaps and eating bon-bons?"

John simply shook his head, rolled his eyes, and walked away.

Julie once again was left feeling very alone.

As Julie sat on the couch, Satan moved in.

She felt dejected and lost in her thoughts: "Why won't John listen to me?"

Satan amplified her thoughts with: "He'll never listen. He doesn't love you!"

"I feel so alone," Julie thought.

Satan: "He's going to leave you. Just like your father."

"I'd be better off alone," Julie cried to herself.

Satan: "You are alone!"

"I'm done!"

Julie wept alone, her buttons scraped raw, her mind filled with distorted lies, and her marriage in serious trouble.

The other reason we buy in to Satan's lies is they sound relatively believable. 2 Corinthians 11:14 says, "for Satan himself masquerades as an angel of light." The grand deception is that it sounds like it's coming from inside your own head. The new thoughts are so close to your original thoughts—just more intense and exaggerated—that you start to go along with them. As Julie discovered, they sound logical and reasonable, just extreme. But believable nonetheless.

All that a man achieves and all that he fails to achieve is the direct result of his own thoughts.

—JAMES ALLEN

I'm telling you, it is the evil one who is standing next to you whispering these words, desperately trying to get you to agree with his twisted lies and fabrications. Satan's trickery will always sound like an exaggeration of what you were thinking. Two Christian authors make this observation about what Satan does with our negative thinking.

In every fairy tale, the enemy tries to pit the boy and girl against each other. What Satan is hoping to secure from us is an "agreement," a very subtle but momentous shift in us, where we believe the spin, we go with the feeling, and we accept as reality the deception he is presenting. (It always feels so true.) "Just settle for what you have got." "Don't risk being hurt again." Once we buy in to the lie and make the agreement, we come under the spell and come under the influence of that interpretation of events. Then it pretty much plays itself out; it becomes self-fulfilling. These agreements begin to define the relationship. They certainly color the way we experience one another. It can be devastating to just let this stuff roll on unchecked and unchallenged.[4]

Do you see how your sworn enemy is trying to take down your marriage by using your own thoughts? Just as Satan writes lies on our hearts, he plants a negative thought—an inception—about your spouse deep within your mind. Once Satan's virus has been planted, the idea will define you, your spouse, and your marriage. Look at some of the most powerful lies the great deceiver attempts to get you to believe:

- Conflict is a sign that your marriage is in trouble.
- You would be happier with someone else.
- God doesn't want you to stay in an unhappy marriage.
- Your spouse wasn't God's plan for you . . . you must have married the wrong person.
- Your spouse doesn't love you as much as you love him or her, and you deserve to be loved.
- You tried, but you just can't do this anymore. It's time to move on.
- Your marriage is only going to get worse.
- You are the only one trying to fix your marriage.
- This is too hard . . . marriage shouldn't be this difficult.
- It's no one's fault . . . you've just fallen out of love.[5]

Satan uses these negative beliefs to kill, steal, and destroy a marriage. Does this work? Just ask Sydney.

Because of his job, recreational activities, and the time he spent with "the guys," my husband wasn't home much. When he was home, his attention was riveted to the TV. I was extremely lonely, and I resented his lack of attention to me and our family. We had married at a young age, and I wondered if I had missed something better. I frequently dwelled upon my dissatisfaction with my marriage. Constantly comparing my spouse to fictional men gave me a deeply critical spirit so that nothing he did was good enough. I expected him to make me happy, and I felt sorry for myself when he disappointed me. *Surely other men would treat me better,* I thought. To soothe my self-pity, I escaped deeper into inappropriate thoughts, relishing attention from other men.

When I sensed my youth waving good-bye in my late 20s, I panicked. *I deserve more than this,* I thought, *and pretty soon it's going to be too late to find it!* I was sure that I was a much better wife than my husband deserved, and I believed that some more compatible guy would jump at the chance to love me. I couldn't stand the thought that I might never be happy and fulfilled (by my own definition) in this life. All the people in the movies found their perfect matches; I wanted to discover the "happily ever after" I deserved, too.[6]

I want to make something very clear. I'm not suggesting that all of our negative thoughts are implanted by the evil one. Sydney's husband made some poor choices that carried very real consequences; they weren't simply planted in her mind, and she didn't make them up. Their marriage had some issues that both people needed to address. What I am encouraging you to consider, however, is the possibility that Satan uses our mind as a sort of petri dish. Remember this from your old high school science lab? A petri dish is a shallow glass or plastic round dish where cells, bacteria, fungus, and viruses are grown and studied. The evil one uses our mind, like you would a petri dish, to plant and grow seeds of extreme thinking that lead to helplessness and hopelessness.

You are today where your thoughts have brought you;
you will be tomorrow where your thoughts take you.

—JAMES ALLEN

Perhaps many of these lies and distorted messages are already deeply rooted in your marriage. In the same way that you deal with the lies written on your heart, you must fight back!

FIGHTING SATAN'S INCEPTIONS

So how do we fight negative thinking? I do not advocate some kind of Pollyanna mentality, in which we, like the movie character, sit around and play the "glad game"—looking for something to be glad about in every unpleasantness. We cannot sit around wishing or hoping that our spouse will change truly negative behaviors. But we do need to consider that his or her motives may be more positive than we have previously imagined. We must learn to replace negative thoughts with the truth. We need to do what Romans 12:2 says: "Do not be conformed to the pattern of this world, but be transformed by the renewing of your mind." Let me suggest several practical steps toward renewing your mind and battling negative thinking.

Step 1:
Identify the Inception

The first line of defense is to notice that you are being victimized by an evil inception—damaging thoughts (lies) solely intended to destroy your marriage. Listen to these Christian authors:

> The first thing we want you to do is recognize what is happening as the enemy presents an agreement, and give it no quarter. Fight it, resist it, and send it packing to the outer reaches of hell. Recognize what is at stake here. The kingdom teeters on the hundred small choices we make every day.[7]

We must begin by acknowledging the presence of negative thinking. It's imperative that you notice how Satan attempts to cause a rift in your relationship. Spend some time with the Lord and ask Him specific questions:

- How is Satan trying to twist my mind against my spouse?
- Have I made any negative interpretations that Satan is trying to exaggerate or intensify?
- What lies is Satan trying to convince me are true about my spouse right now?
- What deception have I bought into about my marriage?

I realized one of Satan's inceptions the other day. I was sitting at the kitchen table working on this very chapter. It was late in the evening, and the kids were already asleep. I was writing away and enjoying the peace and quiet. Erin had been out with some girlfriends and walked into the kitchen. Her eyes quickly spotted dirty dishes in the sink. In frustration, she began to rinse the plates, cups, and silverware and loudly crammed them into the dishwasher.

"Do you guys think that I'm the maid?" she stated matter-of-factly and to no one in particular. My instant vision of my wife in one of those little French-maid outfits didn't help me go to the place of compassion that I think she was looking for.

That was the extent of our interaction. She really wasn't that upset—more frustrated at coming home to a dirty kitchen. We didn't really even experience a good old-fashioned Reactive Cycle. But Satan tried to plant one of his inceptions into my mind.

I sat there and thought, "Wow, the nerve! She was out with her friends while I was home with the kids. Did she even ask how my evening was? No. Did she ask how the kids did while she was out having fun with her friends? No! If she had, I would have told her about the big fight that Garrison and Murphy had. I would have shared about the huge cup of water that Annie spilled all over the living room rug." (Let's not talk about what a toddler was doing with a big cup of water in the living room in the first place . . . this is my tirade!)

Thinking is the grand originator of our experience.

—WILLIAM JAMES

Do you see how the evil one takes our initial negative thought and spins it to the extreme? Remember, he is like an evil stage director, feeding you line after line. Lie after lie. The more I heard these things in my mind, the more I agreed with the twisted reasoning! "Yes, she didn't even notice that I folded the laundry or that I picked up Garrison's messy room! Why does she seem to focus on what I don't do? It's not like I can get everything done in one evening. I have a marriage book to write, after all! She doesn't appreciate the things that I do for the family! I worked all day and then encouraged her to go out that night. Doesn't she think that I could use a break? Doesn't she realize that I'm exhausted as well? I can't believe the first thing she does when she comes home is criticize me for the one thing I didn't do. I'm sick of her critical attitude!"

You might be sitting there thinking, "You got all of that from Erin's one little comment?"

Yes, but I wasn't alone. My sworn enemy was only too happy to assist. The inception was successfully implanted to grow and fester deep within my mind and heart, with one purpose—to cause division and strife between me and my wife. But not tonight!

Step 2:
Reject the Inception

Remember, the progression of finding evidence and building a case against our spouse takes place silently in our mind, and we usually don't realize what is happening—we don't notice that negative beliefs are being embedded in our mind toward our spouse.

Thus, we must refuse to let Satan's lies invade our mind. We need to immediately consider these negative thoughts as lies from the evil one. This is exactly what the apostle Paul understood when he wrote, "We demolish arguments and every pretension that sets itself up against the knowledge of God, and we take captive every thought to make it obedient to Christ" (2 Corinthians 10:5). Isn't that an amazing verse? Another word for "pretension" is "deception." We are being told that the way to destroy arguments and deception is to take every one of these negative thoughts captive and make it obedient to Christ.

The ancestor of every action is a thought.

—RALPH WALDO EMERSON

On a practical level, we can reject Satan's inceptions by giving our spouse the benefit of the doubt. Our attitude toward our spouse must be: "I could be wrong." Paul encourages Christians to be mature in their thinking: "Brethren, do not be children in your thinking; yet in evil be babes, but in your thinking be mature" (1 Corinthians 14:20). Mature thinking happens when we understand that we can never be 100 percent correct in how we interpret our spouse's words and behaviors. Even if we think we're 99 percent right, there's always a 1 percent chance that we're wrong. Therefore, it's important that we maintain a "tentative" attitude about the accuracy of our negative conclusions. We must humbly ask ourselves if we're being too negative in an interpretation of our spouse's actions. We need to consider that we are being fed lies from the evil one or that we might have misunderstandings stemming from a different perspective. We must keep an open mind that our assumptions might not be the result of our spouse's negative traits.

I sat there at my kitchen table, embarrassed at the thoughts that had raced through my mind about my precious wife. I realized that I was being attacked by the evil one; I realized that I needed the Holy Spirit to help me. "But the Helper will teach you everything and will cause you to remember all that I told you. This Helper is the Holy Spirit whom the Father will send in my name" (John 14:26; NCV). I know this is silly, but part of me views the Holy Spirit like the robot from the 1960s television series *Lost in Space*. The robot, acting as a surrogate guardian, says, "Danger, Will Robinson!" when the boy is unaware of an impending threat. Like the robot, I want to hear "Danger, Greg Smalley!" in the presence of Satan's attacks on my mind. Once we expose the danger, we need to immediately seek out the truth.

Step 3:
Discover God's Truth

Allow your heavenly Father, the author of truth, to speak to your mind. This is why we've been encouraged to "set your mind on the things above, not on the things that are on earth" (Colossians 3:2).

I prayed for God to give me a picture of my wife through His eyes—to remind me of the truth about who she is. We must apply Philippians 4:6–8 in this moment. The first two verses focus on seeking out God's truth through prayer and petition: "Do not be anxious about anything, but in every situation, by prayer and petition, with thanksgiving, present your requests to God. And the peace of God, which transcends all understanding, will guard your hearts and your minds in Christ Jesus" (Philippians 4:6–7). I love how this passage of Scripture talks about God's peace (which we receive when we encounter His truth): It says that God's peace surpasses all understanding and will guard our heart and mind. That's the key—we need God's truth to act as a sentry, patrolling the area around our heart and mind.

Instead of focusing on the negative, we must also notice what our spouse does that is positive. We need this balanced point of view. Your spouse certainly is already doing some positive things, but you may be unaware of them because of your negative lens. To begin with, watch your spouse and try to regularly notice his or her positive behaviors—the things that bless you, encourage you, please you, and cause you to feel loved. Focusing on these things helps you to break through the barriers that cloud your vision of your mate's good deeds.

It is neither good nor bad, but thinking makes it so.

—WILLIAM SHAKESPEARE

The apostle Paul recognized the importance of this when he wrote: "Finally, brethren, whatever is true, whatever is honorable, whatever is right, whatever is pure, whatever is lovely, whatever is of good repute, if there is any excellence and if anything worthy of praise, let your mind dwell on these things" (Philippians 4:8). It's no accident that Paul started the last part of Philippians 4:6–8 by encouraging us to think about the truth—whatever is *true*. If I pray, "Lord, what is true about Erin?" this is the only way I can fight Satan's inception. "Lord, what is right, honorable, pure, lovely, excellent, and praiseworthy about Erin?" The truth about my wife instantly comes back into focus.

Once I begin to see my wife and marriage through the eyes of my heavenly Father, a peace that surpasses all understanding floods my body. It enables me to substitute a more reasonable response for the negative thoughts. Instead of trying to read our spouse's mind, we need to be open to the possibility that we could be wrong, and seek God's truth. Doing so opens the door for a more positive or reasonable conclusion. For example, when Erin has a certain look on her face and says in a particular tone of voice, "We need to talk," I instantly jump to a negative conclusion. My first thought is usually

"Great, now what have I done wrong? Why am I in trouble?" Suddenly, I feel frustrated and anxious. Satan plants the inception, and I start thinking, "I'm not perfect! Why does Erin always expect perfection? She makes mistakes as well. She's done such-and-such . . ." And I start to think through every little annoyance or frustration that Erin has committed. Suddenly, the evil one has my negative thoughts racing out of control, and I'm ready for war. How might things have been different had I considered other possible conclusions to Erin's "We need to talk" statement? I might not have gotten so agitated and emotionally flooded. I may have entertained the possibility that she wanted to discuss something positive I did (it's conceivable—highly unlikely but possible!). I could have thought that even if Erin was mad, it would last for only a short time. Perhaps God was using Erin to speak truth into my life. Considering other options allows me to take the fourth step.

Step 4:
Check Out the Accuracy of Your Negative Thinking

Even after we entertain the possibility of an alternative explanation for our spouse's behavior, we need to ask them to help us understand their viewpoint. Since we haven't heard their perspective, it's important that we have a conversation about what happened. We need to have an open mind. We must ask our spouse directly so that they can correct any misinterpretations, misunderstandings, or faulty conclusions. It will fix any negative thinking that might have begun to take root in our mind.

I instantly went into our bedroom to find Erin. I wasn't going to give these lies any room to grow and fester in my marriage! "I'm sorry that you had to come home to a dirty kitchen," I apologized. "I know that feels dishonoring to you. But it was discouraging for me that your maid comment seemed to suggest that you only care about what I hadn't accomplished tonight and that you weren't focused on what I had done."

The beauty of checking out the negative thoughts is that you give your spouse the opportunity to clarify his or her words. "I was actually talking about our children," Erin explained, "I don't feel that way about you. I was just frustrated and shouldn't have made the comment. I'm sorry!"

Just as fast as Satan's inception had started, it was gone. "And the truth will set you free" (John 8:32). It's amazing how quickly freedom is delivered and how fast unity is restored when we seek God's truth and check things out with our spouse. Even if Erin had felt like I was treating her like a maid (there's the French-maid thing in my mind again; I like that inception!), then I at least would have been dealing with her actual concern and not the evil one's lie.

THE NEW WORLDVIEW

In the 1999 science fiction action film *The Matrix,* one of the main characters, Morpheus, offers Neo a choice of two pills: a blue one that would return him to his old life and a red pill that would reveal the truth. Neo swallows the red pill and abruptly discovers the truth about his world: a future in which reality, as perceived by most humans, is actually a simulated reality created by machines to pacify and subdue the human population, while their bodies' heat and electrical activity are used as an energy source.[8] At its essence, *The Matrix* is a movie about massive deception. Sound familiar?

I hope this chapter has offered you the red pill—the truth that we have an enemy who wants you to develop negative beliefs about your spouse and marriage. The reality is that Satan will stop at nothing to get you to see your spouse through a negative lens. I encourage you to see the deception for what it is and join the rebellion against the evil one, alongside other people who have been freed from the dreamworld into reality. One of the best ways to care for your marriage is to guard it from becoming infected by negative beliefs. In the words of Morpheus, "Welcome to the new world."

What do you get when you take your emotional buttons, your fight-or-flight reactions, the lies that have been written on your heart and mind, and add them together over the span of many years? You get the most devastating conclusion to the Reactive Cycle: a hardened heart. And a hardened heart can kill a marriage. Keep reading.

Six

The Hardened Heart

The real problem with unhealthy conflict is what it does to your heart. According to the Cleveland Clinic, parts of your heart—the four valves—open and close more than 400,000 times every day.[1] But did you know that your "relational" heart, the vital center of the real you, opens and closes every day as well? Let me explain.

In a marriage, when we get hurt, frustrated, disappointed, or take a spin around the Reactive Cycle, we instantly go into a protective posture, and our heart shuts down into a tight little ball—like one of those roly-poly bugs. The trigger might be a certain negative look, action, word, or phrase. It could be your spouse's tone of voice, shake of the head, roll of the eyes, use of the thumb and forefinger to make an "L." Hopefully, you don't get the throat-slash hand gesture—that's not a good sign!

Feeling undeservedly attacked, you snap back or leave the room. Far more important to realize is that your heart has just shut down.

This is how we protect ourselves. Animals do the same thing out in the wild. Think about a turtle that retreats into its shell when threatened, a skunk that sprays its repugnant odor when danger approaches, or a possum that plays dead. If you think these acts of self-protection are extreme, they don't hold a candle to some other little creatures'. The fulmar (which looks like a seagull) defends itself by projectile-vomiting at an attacker. The bombardier beetle is famous for being able to spray boiling-hot and toxic bodily fluids in the direction of any would-be predator. However, my favorite is the horned lizard: When attacked, it pressures its own sinus cavities until the blood vessels in its eyes burst and it sprays its attacker with blood from its eyes.[2] That would definitely get your spouse's attention!

Hardening of the heart ages people more quickly than hardening of the arteries.

—AUTHOR UNKNOWN

Why do we go into this closed-hearted protection? The main reason is unhealthy conflict. When we get into the Reactive Cycle, it sets you and your spouse up as adversaries. It's now you against your spouse. When you feel like your spouse is your opponent, the relationship feels emotionally unsafe. Whether it's the conflict topic, the negative body language, the buttons that get pushed, or the reactions, all of these things feel unsafe at some level. And the moment we feel unsafe in our marriage, we go into self-protection, our hearts close, and we disconnect from our spouse.

Sadly, this is the opposite of how we were created to be. When

God created us, He planted an irresistible craving to connect with others on a deep emotional level. We have an insatiable longing to be known intimately, for someone to discover the real person inside. When you slowly sound out the word "intimacy," you find *"into me see."* Each of us longs for our spouse to see into the depths of our heart. God placed inside us the desire to be known, wanted, needed, and cherished. He designed us so that we find meaning and completeness in relationships: "The LORD God said, 'It is not good for the man to be alone'" (Genesis 2:18). We were all designed to relate significantly and deeply with one another; we were all designed to become one with our spouse. Thus, God created our heart to be open. Openness is the default setting of our hearts. Yet many of us struggle with various aspects of intimacy because it requires openness. When our heart is open, we are vulnerable. It's easy to get hurt, upset, or frustrated. So when something negative or painful happens, we feel emotionally threatened, and we shut down to protect ourselves.

By the way, it's not just unhealthy conflict that causes your heart to shut down. Take a look at some additional reasons why a heart may close:

- Financial problems
- Depression or anxiety
- Busyness and the hectic pace of life. As a matter of fact, in the Chinese Mandarin written language, the symbol for "busyness" is made up of two other words: heart + killing
- Feeling tired or not getting enough sleep
- Chaos or stress
- Unrealistic expectations
- Lies written on your heart
- Negative self-talk (*I'm such an idiot!* or *I'll never be able to do that!*)

- Feeling hungry or having low blood sugar
- Fear
- Loneliness
- Frustration or anger
- Dealing with grief
- Sin: "When Pharaoh saw that the rain and hail and thunder had stopped, he sinned again: He and his officials hardened their hearts" (Exodus 9:34)

When these things happen (i.e., financial problems, you get cut off by another driver, etc.), your buttons get pushed, you react (fight or flight), and your heart instantly closes up into a tight little ball.

How can you tell that your spouse has a closed heart? Here are some signs that a heart is shut down:

- No eye contact
- Folded or crossed arms
- Avoiding touch
- Other negative body language
- Withdrawal
- Resentment
- Attack mode
- Insensitivity
- Selfishness
- Unforgiveness
- Emotionally distant
- Faithlessness
- Hopelessness
- Anger

How would your spouse and family know when your heart is shut down? I asked my kids if there was anything I do that warns them my heart is closed. I wasn't sure what they'd say, but I was shocked when they all looked at one another and smiled.

"No way," I said. "What do I do?"

All three answered the same. "We know that we need to walk very carefully," they explained, "when you get real quiet and bite your lower lip."

The worst prison would be a closed heart.

—POPE JOHN PAUL II

I started to object until I noticed that I was actually biting my lip. Apparently, when I get upset and my heart shuts down, I start to gnaw on parts of my own body. And you thought you had problems! The key is to better understand what it looks like or feels like when your heart is closed. Is it something from the above list, or is it something else?

One major problem with a closed heart is that our fight-or-flight reactions are going to be more intense and more relationally harmful (i.e., infidelity, rage, cruel behavior, drug/alcohol abuse, pornography, lying, etc.). Author Adam Anderson puts it this way, "When hearts are closed, we more readily become defensive. We are more likely to become angry and display shortsightedness. We tend to be more prideful and selfish. . . . We are less likely to have meaningful interactions in our relationships."[3]

During the Reactive Cycle, I know my heart has shut down when

I get really defensive and become solely committed to making sure Erin knows that I didn't do anything wrong—that I didn't fail or make a mistake. I desperately attempt to explain my actions or rationalize my choices. But when my heart is closed and I react, I'm not a safe person to be around. Not only am I likely to say or do something that will hurt my wife, I'm unsafe because I'm consumed with me. I'm trying to soothe my hurt feelings (buttons), and I'm not really thinking about Erin. I've lost perspective. This is the other main problem with a closed heart. Again, think animal. When a turtle's head is retracted or the roly-poly bug is curled up tight, it can't see beyond itself. The world becomes dark.

King David spoke about not being able to see when his heart was troubled: "For troubles without number surround me; my sins have overtaken me, and I cannot see . . . and my heart fails within me" (Psalm 40:12). When our heart is shut down, we become confused. Our judgment is clouded. Awareness, insight, and discernment are nonexistent.

In this closed state, we often end up making brain-only decisions that are heartless. It's so easy to rationalize choices when we lack perspective and are using just our brain. This is why good people are capable of making terrible choices when their heart is shut down. We've all heard someone say, "He was the last person on earth I thought would do that" or "I never thought she was capable of doing that." Listen to Andrea's explanation of how she ended up having an affair:

I never thought I was the kind of person who would have an affair. I was raised in a strong Christian home and believed firmly in the moral values from my childhood. I loved my husband. I didn't wake up one morning and lose everything I believed in. Satan worked in my heart and mind gradually, feeding me a lie over time. I wasn't capable of having an affair on day one. But after that, I was. I became capable.[4]

We become capable of practically anything when our heart is closed. And the longer our heart remains shut down, the more likely it is that our heart will harden. And a hardened heart can kill a marriage.

THE HARDENED HEART

Certainly, the Reactive Cycle is frustrating. It's a complete waste of time, it doesn't get us what we want relationally, we may feel stuck, we may hate the fight-or-flight reactions, and our heart shuts down. When our heart is closed, we lack perspective and are more likely to make poor or hurtful decisions. But the real danger is allowing our heart to stay shut down. Over time, the heart that is closed will begin to slowly fossilize or harden. The Christian music group Casting Crowns sang about this in their popular song "Slow Fade." Listen to the lyrics:

> *Families never crumble in a day*
> *It's a slow fade, it's a slow fade*
> *It's a slow fade to a hard heart.*[5]

This is exactly what happened to Mike after nearly thirty years of marriage. Listen to his ex-wife, Michele, explain the slow fade of their marriage.

My husband left me so he could live with a co-worker he's been having an affair with for at least six months. He never told me he was unhappy. I always felt so fortunate that I had him for my husband. I did notice some subtle changes over the past three years. He became less affectionate and seemed to lose his desire for me. He started to sleep downstairs more often and made excuses like "I have sleeping problems" or "My asthma is bothering me."

I never doubted his love for me because it had always been so constant. The past six months he seemed to really emotionally withdraw. He stopped sharing the details of his life and quit asking about me. During the Christmas holidays, he didn't even really try to connect with our grown daughter, who was home visiting. My daughter and I were so distraught. She even started to cry and asked what was wrong, but Mike didn't appear to know how to respond. Of course, I was beside myself and begged him tell me what was wrong. I decided to take him to a resort to Costa Rica to help him de-stress. It was right before the trip that he confessed the affair.

"I'm having an affair with someone at work," he impassionately explained. "I'm totally obsessed with her and I'm afraid I will lose her to another man if I don't leave you."

I never thought my husband was capable of infidelity or such deception. I asked him if he was willing to give up his family for her, and he replied, "I think so. I just don't love you anymore."[6]

It's a slow fade to a hard heart.

The dictionary defines "hardened" as cold, insensitive, unfeeling, and unyielding. The phrase "hard heart" appears more than thirty-six times throughout the Bible: ". . . but whoever hardens their heart falls into trouble" (Proverbs 28:14). Here is a great description of a hardened heart.

A hardened heart keeps pace with the world more than it does with Jesus. It doesn't seek out or listen to Godly counsel or wisdom from the Bible. It stops rhythmically communicating with God and seals off the work of the Holy Spirit. It loses faith in God's abilities to bless us and work miracles. It is selfish and sows bitterness, anger, resentment, jealousy, malice, discontent and other evils. It causes more harm than good. It calls evil good and good evil and justifies evil actions. It silences the conscience and suppresses truth. It does not desire forgiveness, healing, faith and hope in God. It substitutes pleasure for righteousness. A hardened heart, without treatment, could fall away from God entirely and be left spiritually corrupted and bankrupt, deprived of spiritual nutrients and every good and amazing thing God had planned for it.[7]

A hardened, dead heart is what the evil one is determined to create, and he will stop at nothing to accomplish this strategy.

For every beauty there is an eye somewhere to see it.
For every truth there is an ear somewhere to hear it.
For every love there is a heart somewhere to receive
it.

—IVAN PANIN

Relationally, you can always tell that someone's heart is hardening when he or she uses a phrase like "I just don't love you anymore." It's like the Righteous Brothers song, "You've Lost That Lovin'

Feelin.'" I've heard it hundreds of times from the couples that I've counseled. As a matter of fact, this is the most common question asked during the first session: "Can you help us feel in love again?" The question can take many forms and slight variations:

- How can I restore my marriage?
- Can I ever love him again?
- Is it too late to rekindle our love?
- How can I bring healing and restoration of love and trust to my marriage?
- Is it possible to rediscover the passion we once had for each other?
- Can you help me feel like something besides his roommate?

When I counsel a married couple and hear one spouse talking about not feeling "in love" with his or her mate, it's vital to help that person look at the situation differently. Instead of talking about love and suggesting twelve or so steps to reignite the passion in their marriage, they need to understand something very important about love.

Despite what our culture wants us to believe, love is not about magic or chemistry. It's not something that happens as the result of some invisible power. All that love we talk about, write about, and sing about—none of it comes from us. We do not create love. God is the author of love. "Dear friends, let us love one another, for love comes from God . . . because God is love" (1 John 4:7–8). The only reason we love at all is because God first poured His love into our hearts, "We love because he first loved us" (1 John 4:19). All love comes from God; we do not generate a single drop. When I open my heart to God, He then fills my heart abundantly full of His love. If you don't believe me, listen to your heavenly Father's words: "And I pray that you, being rooted and established in love, may have power, together with all the Lord's holy people, to grasp how wide and long and high and deep is the love of Christ, and to know this love that surpasses knowledge—that you may be filled to the measure of all the fullness of God" (Ephesians 3:16–20).

Have a heart that never hardens, a temper that never tires, a touch that never hurts.

—CHARLES DICKENS

I love the phrase "filled to the measure of all the fullness of God." Isn't it a cool thought, that God wants our heart filled with all the love that He has to offer? The process of love continues once our heart is full of God's love. We simply open our heart and allow God's love to flow out to our spouse's heart.

When I say "I love you" to my wife, that wonderful feeling of love is God flowing through my open heart. This is the very reason why King Solomon warned us to "Above all else, guard your heart, for it is the wellspring of life" (Proverbs 4:23). The life-giving wellspring that flows from our open heart is God's love. This is why we have to guard our hearts from closing, and worse, from hardening. It's heartbreaking to hear stories of people whose hearts have slowly faded to stone, like Rachael, who shared her diary during counseling.

I have been with my husband for seven years now. Though I am committed to this marriage and to my duties as a wife and mother, and I am not contemplating divorce, I don't feel love for him and don't feel physical desire for him. Frankly, I don't find him to be a lovable person. And because I feel so terribly overburdened with responsibilities of supplementing our income, housekeeping, and parenting, I have strong feelings of resentment that get in the way of any desire for intimacy with him. I can't bear to kiss him and kind of have to work up a mental fantasy to engage in physical intimacy. I know this is a cruel thing to say, but I have lost all love for my husband.[8]

When people say they don't feel love for their spouse, the problem isn't the love. God's love is always available. King David recognized this when he wrote, "The earth is filled with your love, Lord" (Psalm 119:64). God's love is all around us—it's like air. When our heart is open, He flows through us. Even actress and jewelry designer Jane Seymour understands this truth. (Remember the show *Dr. Quinn, Medicine Woman?*) She has an entire line of jewelry with Kay Jewelers called Open Hearts, and her slogan is "If your heart is open, love will always find its way in." If Dr. Quinn gets it, how can we have missed the importance of an open heart?

When one spouse doesn't feel love toward the other, it isn't a sign that he or she is cold-blooded, or that the other spouse is unlovable, or that the marriage is damaged, or that they're not "soul mates." It just means that their hearts are growing hard. This is what they really need to be concerned about. This is what I quickly help the couples I'm working with understand. It's a heart issue, not a love issue.

Spiteful words can hurt your feelings, but silence breaks your heart.

—PHYLLIS MCGINLEY

One of the things that I learned over my years of working with marriages in crisis is that every failed relationship stems from a hardened heart. This is exactly what Jesus explained when asked about divorce: "Moses permitted you to divorce your wives because your hearts were hard" (Matthew 19:8). That's such a fascinating verse. I don't think I ever would have come up with permitting divorce because of a hardened heart. But the reality is that a hardened heart is the real destroyer of marriage. Max Lucado agrees: "A hard heart ruins not only your life, but your marriage as well. Jesus identified the hard heart as the wrecking ball of a marriage. When one or both people in a marriage harden their heart, they sign its death certificate."[9]

But the problem is that people don't realize this fact. They say the issue is that they've fallen out of love, or they blame their marriage problems on other issues. Just look at the list of common reasons people cite for divorce.

- We have no money.
- I hate the way he parents.
- I can't stand her personality quirks.
- All he does is work.
- We rarely have sex.
- We fight and argue constantly.
- He had an extramarital affair.
- I recently met my soul mate.
- We're not compatible.
- She has too many unrealistic expectations.
- I have nothing in common with him.
- I feel like I'm living with a roommate.
- My in-laws are driving me crazy.

Is the problem really irreconcilable differences, or is it a heart issue? The issues on this list will exacerbate the problems in a hurting marriage, but they are secondary issues. The real trouble is a heart that has turned to stone.

> After some discussion with a friend, I just realized that I am apathetic toward my marriage. I hate to admit it, but . . . my marital responsibilities are carried out due to obligation and not desire. I am neither passionate nor motivated to improve the relationship. My communication is the bare minimum. This really came to light a few weeks ago, when I picked up a book to improve my relationship but never made it past the first chapter and lost interest. I hate to be apathetic, but I just do not know where I want the relationship to go.[10]

Apathy is far from God's desire for our marriage. Apathy is the absence of emotions or feelings toward your spouse, when you just don't care anymore and your attitude is "whatever." Some people describe it as coldhearted. When apathy infects a marriage, the contaminated spouse is robbed of joy, passion, and meaning. He or she becomes cynical and pessimistic, believing that nothing can change. Thus, the apathetic person becomes indifferent, disinterested, and unresponsive to the needs and desires of his or her spouse. The apathetic spouse appears selfish. Sadly, apathy feeds on itself. Selfishness leads to a lack of sympathy or concern for the other person. Once someone no longer cares for or serves his or her spouse, it's not long before the indifference overwhelms the other spouse. Soon the couple starts to believe that the marriage is over.

Take away love, and our earth is a tomb.

—ROBERT BROWNING

When a heart is hardened and apathy has taken root, the person no longer desires a relationship with his or her spouse. Worse, that person almost always disconnects from God as well. This is exactly why King David wrote, "The LORD says, 'Don't harden your hearts as Israel did. . . . They refuse to do what I tell them'" (Psalm 95:8–10; NLT). And that is why Jesus asked his disciples, "Why are you talking about having no bread? Do you still not see or understand? Are your hearts hardened? Do you have eyes but fail to see, and ears but fail to hear? And don't you remember?" (Mark 8:17–18). A hardened heart impedes a person's ability to recognize God's voice and understand what he is saying. Author Doug Apple explains:

> When your heart is hard, it is not open to God. You do not want to listen to God. You don't want to hear His word. You don't want to know about His plan or His design. And you certainly don't want to listen to any correction. A hard heart towards God separates us from God. It separates us from His wisdom, which allows us to become ignorant. It separates us from His light, which puts us in darkness."[11]

When our hearts are fossilized and we are separated from God, we can't hear or won't listen to His voice. Sadly, we make devastating choices with lasting consequences. A hardened heart often ignores what God says about relationship problems and usually disregards God's will for his or her marriage. "He has blinded their eyes and hardened their hearts, so they can neither see with their eyes, nor understand with their hearts" (John 12:40).

Before you make a decision about your marriage, open your heart. You can't possibly make a good decision, much less a Christlike decision, about your marriage when your heart is closed or hardened. Ed Price, in his book *The Loving Heart*, says:

The hardened heart is a stubborn attitude that leads a person to reject God's will. It is an act of defiance; one of ignorance. Self-control and humbleness is the way of Christ, not self-righteousness. But their hardened hearts will not accept this truth. They believe what their hardened hearts want to believe. When He allows personal tragedy to strike, hearts may harden against Him. When He leads us on paths where we do not want to go, that may harden hearts.[12]

One of the most painful experiences in marriage is when a heart hardens. And that is the greatest threat of a Reactive Cycle left unbridled and allowed to run rampant in a marriage. The journey to a hardened heart happens when a couple is unable to successfully manage arguments and disagreements. Instead of being able to work through conflict, a couple begins to deal with things separately. Since they can't talk about their problems, they silently wallow in their pain or seek out others who will listen. Over time, they begin to lead parallel lives. As this relational Grand Canyon widens, loneliness sets in. And when you feel lonely, the end is near. It's what the Tin Man says in *The Wizard of Oz:* "It was a terrible thing to undergo, but during the year I stood there, I had time to think that the greatest loss I had known was the loss of my heart. While I was in love, I was the happiest man on earth; but no one can love who has not a heart, and so I am resolved to ask Oz to give me one." The good news is that we don't have to follow the yellow brick road to find Oz. Our heart is healed by the God who heals the brokenhearted and binds up their wounds (Psalm 147:3).

In a full heart there is room for everything, and in an empty heart there is room for nothing.

—ANTONIO PORCHIA

HEALING THE HARDENED HEART

We are told three times in the book of Hebrews to "harden not your heart" (Hebrews 3:8, 3:15, and 4:7). It's almost like Paul is trying to tell us something! The question is, what is the state of your heart toward your spouse? Perhaps unhealthy conflict has closed your heart. Maybe there have been years of prolonged hurt and frustration so that your heart has hardened like Brandon's, who explained this to me in one of our sessions (paraphrased):

> I know this is a cruel thing to say, but I have lost all feeling for my wife. I appreciate that she is a very good mom to my children, but how do I break it to her where she will understand that her husband no longer loves her? Should I continue to pretend I love her as I did when I married her twelve years ago and when I had two beautiful children with her? Should I wait till the kids grow older and then ask for a divorce? Should I stay or should I go? They say honesty is important in marriage, but how can I do this without breaking her heart? How can I make her understand that I just don't care anymore? I just don't love her.[13]

Satan desperately wants Brandon focused on the wrong thing—a perceived lack of love for his wife. But this is the great deception. Satan will try to get us to believe that falling out of love is evidence that our marriage is over. Don't buy this lie for one more second. See the real problem for what it is: Your heart is closed or hardened. The healing process begins when you listen to the apostle Paul's advice: "Today, if you hear his voice, do not harden your hearts." (Hebrews 4:7). "His voice" is the voice of your heavenly Father.

REND YOUR HEART

Whatever the condition, the Lord wants to heal your heart. "'Even now,' declares the LORD, 'return to me with all your heart. . . . Rend your heart and not your garments. Return to the LORD your God, for he is gracious and compassionate, slow to anger and abounding in love, and he relents from sending calamity'" (Joel 2:12–13). This is an amazing verse. I love to be reminded of God's grace, compassion, patience, and abundant love. The prophet Joel is trying to tell the tribe of Judah that they can open their hearts to God because He is safe.

But what does "rend your heart" mean? Throughout the Bible, there are many examples of people deliberately tearing their clothing as a physical expression of grief—they were literally saying "it tears me up."[14] To rend something is to tear or split it apart into pieces. In this verse, instead of our clothes, we are being told to tear our hearts in order that we might return to the Lord.

God is not only safe, He is also patient; He will not break through the closed door of your heart. In Revelation 3:20, He makes this clear: "Here I am! I stand at the door and knock. If anyone hears my voice and opens the door, I will come in."

The first move is yours. There are times when a broken bone

can heal only when it is rebroken. Your hardened heart must be cracked open to allow God's healing love to penetrate. Rend open your heart so the Lord can preform a miracle. He makes this promise: "I will sprinkle clean water on you, and you will be clean; I will cleanse you from all your impurities and from all your idols. I will give you a new heart and put a new spirit in you; I will remove from you your heart of stone and give you a heart of flesh. And I will put my Spirit in you and move you to follow my decrees and be careful to keep my laws" (Ezekiel 36:25–27). He promises to heal our heart if we open it to him: "He has blinded their eyes and hardened their hearts, so they can neither see with their eyes, nor understand with their hearts, nor turn—and I would heal them" (John 12:40). "And I would heal them." Drink His promise deep into your heart. Max Lucado writes, "For God so loved the world. . . . This hard-hearted, stiff-necked world. We stick our noses where we shouldn't; still, he pursues us. We run from the very one who can help, but he doesn't give up. He loves. He pursues. He persists. And, every so often, a heart starts to soften.[15] Is your heart hard? Take it to your Father.

<hr />

Seeds, like hearts, must open to grow.

—CAROL HOROS

<hr />

You don't have to live with a hardened heart. You are only a prayer away from a more tender heart. Pray these healing words: *Lord, my heart has failed and I have wandered far from the life you want for me. The pain of losing my heart has been one of the greatest losses that I've ever known. I do not want a heart that is closed or hardened to you. Lord, fill my heart full with your love. I desperately want the eyes and ears of my heart fixed upon you. I rend my heart fully open to you today. Lord, remove from me a heart of stone and give me a heart of flesh. Amen.*

ASK GOD TO TOUCH YOUR HEART

"Create in me a pure heart, O God" (Psalm 51:10). What a powerful prayer. God can heal your heart, no matter the condition. You just need to ask. God can penetrate your heart through praise and worship music, prayer, the Bible, a sermon, humility, and gratitude. "For the eyes of the LORD range throughout the earth to strengthen those whose hearts are fully committed to him" (2 Chronicles 16:9). Ask God to heal your hardened heart. He is so faithful. In response to King Solomon's prayer for wisdom, God said, "I will do what you have asked. I will give you a wise and discerning heart. ... Moreover, I will give you what you have not asked for" (1 Kings 3:12–13). I love that God will do what you ask, but He will also give you what you don't even know to request. "We do not know what we ought to pray for, but the Spirit himself intercedes for us with groans that words cannot express" (Romans 8:26). Your heavenly Father knows exactly what your heart needs: "For your father knows what you need before you ask him" (Matthew 6:8).

God will heal your heart if you ask. "I will give them one heart, and I will put a new spirit within you; and I will take the stony heart out of their flesh, and will give them a heart of flesh" (Ezekiel 11:19). A soft heart of flesh is all God needs to begin the healing and restoration of your marriage.

If God can raise the dead, He can absolutely resurrect a lifeless marriage. I've witnessed the miracle happen in relationships countless times. Truly, there is hope for you!

Let's turn our attention to how we open our hearts in the middle of the Reactive Cycle.

Seven

Opening Your Heart

I trust it's now crystal-clear that conflict in marriage is inevitable. Start with a self-centered man and a self-centered woman with unique personalities and different family backgrounds. Mix in some sensitive emotional buttons that get pushed easily, add some negative habits and interesting quirks, include a collection of unrealistic expectations, all happening in the midst of life's daily trials. Take one guess what happens. You got it—conflict! It's unavoidable and necessary, no matter how long you've been married.

Every marriage, even those that are the healthiest, experiences the occasional argument or disagreement. I'm not suggesting that you get used to fighting; I hate it when Erin and I fight. But I'm hopeful that you've come to realize that healthy conflict is a doorway into the deepest levels of intimacy and connection. This is why marriage experts say that couples who argue and disagree healthfully have more satisfying and fulfilling relationships than those who avoid conflict.

Airing hurt and frustration is one of the healthiest habits a couple can develop within a relationship. Marriage expert John Gottman provides some great insight into this truth:

> If there's one lesson I've learned in my years of research into marital relationships—having interviewed and studied more than 200 couples over 20 years—it is that a lasting marriage results from a couple's ability to resolve the conflicts that are inevitable in any relationship. Many couples tend to equate a low level of conflict with happiness and believe the claim "we never fight" is a sign of marital health. But I believe we grow in our relationships by reconciling our differences. That's how we become more loving people and truly experience the fruits of marriage.[1]

As the title of this book suggests, how a couple manages quarrels and disputes is a key factor in determining their success in marriage. If we allow the Reactive Cycle to spin around unchecked, we are in serious trouble. When our buttons get pushed and we react, it makes our marriage feel unsafe. When we feel unsafe, our heart shuts down, and we ultimately disconnect from our spouse. If this pattern continues over time, our closed heart hardens. And a hardened heart can be the demise of a marriage.

The possibilities are numerous once we decide to act and not react.

—GEORGE BERNARD SHAW

My goal is to teach you a process of dealing with whatever difficulty you will face in your marriage. It's like the old Chinese proverb: "Give a man a fish and you feed him for a day. Teach a man to fish and you feed him for a lifetime." I don't want to give you the answers to resolving one problem. I want to help you to successfully manage all your disagreements.

Where do we begin the process of breaking the Reactive Cycle? How do we end the cycle of unhealthy conflict? I routinely pose this type of question to couples at my marriage seminar: How do you stop an argument once it has started? The most common answer is probably the worst advice we could give to a couple in conflict. Can you guess the answer?

Communication! In essence, the advice goes like this: "When you're in the middle of an argument, you need to sit down and calmly talk about the issues in a healthy and productive manner." This sounds like great counsel, doesn't it?

Here's why it's problematic: When was the last time you and your spouse had a disagreement, a time when you were spinning around in the Reactive Cycle? Were you able to have a productive conversation? Honestly, when your buttons are pushed and your heart is closed, are you capable of having healthy, Christlike communication with your spouse? It's not helpful to tell a couple in conflict that they just need to talk things through. Over the years, I've heard some interesting advice suggesting what we should do in the middle of an argument in order to communicate in a productive manner:

- Try to hold hands while talking.
- Pay attention to your partner as you fight.
- Look into each other's eyes as you discuss problems.
- Finish the fight; don't go to bed angry.

- Maintain as much tender physical contact as possible.
- Let your spouse have the last word.
- Take three minutes to say what's on your mind.
- Think positive thoughts about your spouse.
- Pray in the middle of your fight.

It's not that I don't like these rules for fair fighting. I like the spirit of the tips very much. In a perfect world, I wish we could behave in such compassionate ways during an argument. However, quite frankly, these things rarely work for the average couple. I never see them happening in my office or even in my living room. When buttons have been pushed and hearts are closed, it's practically impossible to have a healthy, kindhearted conversation. The problem is that when we are hurt or upset and our heart is shut down, not only are we relationally unsafe (fight-or-flight reactions), but we lack perspective and insight. Therefore, instead of trying to accomplish things that seem completely unrealistic for the average person in the middle of the Reactive Cycle, I'd rather encourage couples to do something else before the fight that will set them up to have a great conversation.

Action springs not from thought but from a readiness for responsibility.

—DIETRICH BONHOEFFER

THE LOG IN YOUR EYE

The way to break the Reactive Cycle was actually given to us by Jesus during the Sermon on the Mount. "How can you say to your brother, 'Let me take the speck out of your eye,' when all the time there is a plank in your own eye? You hypocrite, first take the plank out of your own eye, then you will see clearly to remove the speck from your brother's eye" (Matthew 7:2–5). So, how do we put Jesus' wise counsel into action?

The verse above is all about personal responsibility. God has made it a clear theme throughout the Scriptures.

You hypocrite, first take the plank out of your own eye. (Matthew 7:5)

Search me, God, and know my heart. (Psalm 139:23)

For each one should carry his own load. (Galatians 6:5)

If it is possible, as far as it depends on you, live at peace with everyone. (Romans 12:18)

Hopefully, you've noticed the thread in the verses above: you. Our ultimate goal is to deal with the log in our own eye by taking full personal responsibility for our feelings and actions. This means that we refuse to focus on our spouse and stop thinking, "If only my spouse would say this" or "If only my spouse would do that." Instead, we decide, "I can't change my spouse, but I can change how I react." Personal responsibility requires that we look at our own side of the equation. It means we say to ourselves, "My buttons, my responsibility. Instead of reacting by fighting or 'flighting,' I'm going to take responsibility and get my heart back open. Instead of trying to get my spouse to act a certain way, I'm going to focus on me."

Unity without diversity leads to uniformity.

—WARREN WIERSBE

It's human nature to blame others or try to change them. Just take a look at the very first Reactive Cycle on record. When Adam and Eve were caught eating the fruit, Adam attempted to blame his wife for his poor choice, "The woman you put here with me—she gave me some fruit from the tree, and I ate it" (Genesis 3:12). Like Adam, when we are hurt or frustrated, we want to focus on our spouse and desperately attempt to change how he or she treats us. We attempt in many unhealthy ways (our reactions) to force our spouse to stop pushing our buttons. However, every time we attempt to control our spouse or blame him/her for our feelings or behaviors ("You make me feel _____" or "I wouldn't have done _____ if you hadn't done _____"), we give him/her the power to determine our happiness, success, worth, identity, adequacy, lovability, or whatever. But this approach seems to succeed only in triggering our spouse's buttons, which in turn accelerates the Reactive Cycle. We end up feeling hurt and disconnected, and ultimately, our marriage suffers. Blaming others for our own choices didn't work for Adam, and it won't work for us. So what's the alternative?

Man's last freedom is his freedom to choose how he will react in any given situation.

—VIKTOR FRANKL

Conflict is a fact of life. We will never stop people from pushing our buttons. However, we do have a choice in what we do afterward. This is exactly what Max Lucado suggested: "Conflict is inevitable, but combat is optional."[2] We do have control over how we choose to react to adversity. I'm certain you've heard of personal responsibility, but few of us have been taught how to live out this powerful concept within our marriage. So, let me make personal responsibility practical, all the way down to its most basic question: What do you do when your buttons are pushed?

WHEN YOUR BUTTONS ARE PUSHED . . .

The next time your buttons get pushed, you must *first* deal with you—the log in your own eye. The key is to get your heart open so that you can *respond* to your spouse. This is very important—the primary goal here. When our heart is open, we are less likely to react and more likely to respond to our spouse. Responding feels safe, and his or her heart is more likely to stay open when we create safety.

Let me tell you a comical story as a backdrop for explaining how we break the Reactive Cycle. It's actually a time when I almost got beat up by a biker, and I'm not talking about the Tour de France type. I mean the biker who rides a Harley—the Hells Angels type!

A number of years ago, my family was getting ready to fly out of town on vacation. I don't know about you, but I hate getting ready for trips. By the time we're finally driving, everyone is irritable and exhausted from packing and dealing with all the last-minute details. For this particular trip, we had to fly out of an airport that we had never been to. And because Murphy's Law reigns supreme any time you are late for the airport, as soon as we started driving, I noticed that we were out of gas.

"Erin!" I yelled. "You never got gas!"

"I thought you were going to do that!"

Yes, the cycle was already starting to build momentum.

As I pulled into the gas station, I was struck by how many motor-cycles there were. They were everywhere. It looked like a biker con-vention. There was every shape and size of motorcycle known to man.

"Are we having a Hells Angels convention?" I asked Erin.

"I think our town is hosting something for bikers raising money for some charity," Erin explained.

I felt like I was driving through an obstacle course as I weaved among bikers. I finally found a spot and pulled right behind a beau-tiful motorcycle. It was pulling a small trailer with matching colors. I must admit it looked impressive—and expensive.

Speaking of "expensive," after topping off the tank of our SUV, I whistled at the rising costs of fuel and how much I had spent. I was either distracted by that or the fact that my kids were now fighting in the backseat, because as I pulled away from the gas pump, I no-ticed out of the corner of my eye that the beautiful (and expensive) motorcycle in front of me had fallen over.

"That can't be good," I said to Erin. "Someone is going to be very upset."

It hadn't dawned on me that I had knocked the bike over. I got out to look at why the motorcycle had fallen, and that's when I no-ticed that I had rammed the trailer with my SUV.

It is far more important to be the right kind of person than it is to marry the right person. In short, whether you married the right or wrong person is primarily up to you.

—ZIG ZIGLAR

I stood there for several seconds in complete disbelief. I quickly scanned the parking lot to see if anyone had noticed my blunder. Since I didn't see any Hells Angels running my way, I figured "no harm, no foul." I could simply right the fallen bike and we'd be on our way.

Well, let me just tell you, those bikes are insanely heavy. I couldn't budge it. I instantly started to bead up with sweat. I was going to have to go in and confess to someone—hopefully, someone who wasn't packing heat.

Talk about feeling like a complete failure. Let me tell you that many of my buttons were flashing as I walked into the gas station. It was like an alarm had tripped inside my head.

"Does anyone own a new red Honda Gold Wing with a matching trailer?" I timidly asked.

Just my luck, this hulk of a man said, "Why?"

"You're not going to like this," I stammered, "but my pregnant wife . . ." (I'm kidding.) "But I accidentally knocked it over" is what I actually said.

I can't tell you what he said in reaction to my confession. Mainly because I've blocked it out or had never heard some of the words he used. Thank goodness the man's wife (or "woman," as he called her) helped calm him down. I'm not sure what she did, but I do remember her yelling, "You don't want to go back to prison, do you?"

After exchanging insurance information with him and promising that I would never disrespect a man's "hog" like that again, my family and I were back on our way to the airport. However, as you could imagine, we were now severely late and emotionally agitated. I'm telling you this because when I climbed back into the SUV, Erin (trying to be helpful, I'm sure) said, "Make sure you look closely before pulling out this time." I wish I could tell you that I thanked her for the thoughtful concern and assistance, but I'd be lying. Instead, we cycled—big-time!

Is this the reality of marriage—buttons getting pushed, reactions, and hurt? Is this our relational destiny—the Reactive Cycle? Instead of causing disconnection, could I have done something differently that might have brought us closer together instead of further apart? YES! We always have a choice in how we manage disagreements. We have a choice in how we respond or react once our buttons get pushed. In all my work with couples in crisis, I've narrowed down everything that I've learned to three powerful steps to break the Reactive Cycle. As you will see, each step builds on the other toward the ultimate goal: an open heart.

Wherever you go, go with all your heart.

—CONFUCIUS

1. Hit the Pause Button

When you get a button pushed or engage in the Reactive Cycle, the first step is to hit the pause button—like on your TV remote. In these tense moments, it's extremely helpful to create some space, take a break, or call a time-out. The goal is to calm down and allow your stirred-up emotions to settle. If you don't create some type of space, you are more likely to keep reacting and cause further relational damage. This is especially important if your reaction style is on the fight side. James Groesbeck put it this way;

> Rather than avoiding conversation or withdrawing altogether, take time-outs when things get dicey. When you're not making progress by talking, when you feel emotionally exhausted, or when the conversation becomes negative, step back and take a break. Time-outs can help you get a new perspective. Agree to continue the discussion constructively or end it until you and your spouse can handle it well.[3]

Hitting the pause button is all about controlling your behavior before you react. As Jacqueline Schiff put it, "The best remedy for a short temper is a long walk." In the middle of an argument, it can be difficult to control your emotions, and yet you can hold back your words and actions. This is exactly what King Solomon advised when he wrote, "A fool gives full vent to his anger, but a wise man keeps himself under control" (Proverbs 29:11). In the same way, don't say or do something that you will regret later. You don't have to act on your feelings or interpretations.

To accomplish this, you should not only stop talking, but it can also be a good thing to temporarily separate from your spouse. Sometimes our buttons get so massively pushed that we need to physically remove ourselves and create some literal space in order to calm down. Other times we are mildly irritated or frustrated and can quickly refocus emotionally without leaving the room, then re-engage our spouse once we've settled down and our heart is back open.

The experts call this self-soothing, and it's a great skill for managing your buttons when they've been pushed. Self-soothing is the ability to calm or center yourself when confronted with conflict or other stressful situations.[4] Instead of stewing about what your spouse did and how upset you are, using the ability to self-soothe means you can deescalate your heightened emotions and reduce your negative thinking. Here is a list of some specific ideas that will help you calm down:

- Count slowly to 10
- Focus on your breathing and take several deep breaths
- Stand up and stretch your body
- Spend some time in prayer
- Go lie down or rest for a moment
- Exercise—take a walk or go for a jog
- Listen to soothing music (heavy metal may not work!)
- Quote or read your favorite Bible verses
- Clean something
- Do yard work or wash the family car
- Bake something
- Soak in the tub
- Listen to praise and worship music
- Do laundry
- Play with the kids
- Read a book
- Go for a drive

- Call a friend (don't complain about your spouse; instead focus on your feelings)
- Write down how you feel

We all have techniques that can help us to relax. The key is to use what helps you keep yourself under control. Is there something from the above list that would help you calm down, or is it something entirely different? It doesn't matter what it is as long as it has a relaxing effect. How long should you stay in time-out? The key is to stay away long enough to get your heart back open. Actually, marriage researcher John Gottman found that when you heart rate goes above a hundred beats per minute, you are in fight-or-flight mode. It takes about twenty minutes for your heart rate to return to a normal level.[5] Thus, it's critical to take at least a twenty-minute break before you return to the conversation. But you cannot continue to think about the argument or dwell on what your spouse did or said, which is called distress-maintaining thoughts. This is when you stew, simmer, ruminate, or mull over what your spouse did that hurt or frustrated you. It's when you dwell on how much you were hurt or how upset you are. That will never get you to calm down and deescalate your emotions.

Marriage isn't supposed to make you happy and satisfied. It's your job to make your marriage happy and satisfying.

—DIANE SOLLEE

By the way, there will be times when you are someplace that you cannot physically leave (i.e., driving in the car, dinner party, restaurant, church, etc.). If you cannot leave, for whatever reason, create some "internal" space by not talking with, looking at, or interacting with your spouse for however long it takes for you to settle down and relax. While sitting in the car next to Erin, instead of continuing to react to her, I tuned the radio to my favorite praise and worship station. That is what really helps me to deescalate and calm down. Another way I calm myself down is to watch a few minutes of my favorite comedy shows, like *Seinfield* or *The King of Queens*. I've found that laughter calms me down and gets my heart open. Perhaps this is why King Solomon wrote, "A cheerful heart is good medicine" (Proverbs 17:22; NLT). I would argue, however, that the most powerful way to relax and to get our heart open is prayer. Incredible things happen when we pray to our heavenly Father and invite Him to intervene. Remember, when we seek Him, He promises to soften our heart: "I will give you a new heart and put a new spirit in you; I will remove from you your heart of stone and give you a heart of flesh" (Ezekiel 36:26). A softened "heart of flesh" is open and can safely have a productive conversation.

I want to make one important point of clarification about hitting the pause button. Whenever I encourage couples to do this while they're in the Reactive Cycle, I usually hear the spouse of a "flighter" say, "Thanks a lot . . . you just gave my spouse permission to withdraw!" Look on this as a time-out, not a separation. There is a huge difference between withdrawing and a time-out. Withdrawal is when you emotionally "log off" or physically remove yourself to end the fight; there is no benefit to the relationship here. Withdrawal is all about stopping the conflict. Karen Sherman put it this way:

Understand that the genders are truly different in their styles and the actions taken are not intentionally meant to hurt the other. Men need to remember that when they need to take some space, they should let their wives know that they are merely taking a "time-out" for a little while. Women, allow your man to have some breathing room. Don't assume his leave-taking is anything more than temporary.[6]

Withdrawal destroys marriages, but hitting the pause button is when you proactively get away so you open your heart to your spouse. Let your spouse know that you're taking a time-out and not withdrawing. Tell him that you need some time alone to calm down. Let her know that you *will* discuss the issue later, once your heart is back open. Some couples have developed a code word or hand gesture that they use to explain they are not withdrawing but are creating space for a brief amount of time. Over the years, I've heard things like:

- Code red!
- Monkey butt! (Our fifteen-year-old daughter uses this one.)
- I'm at DEFCON One.
- I'm getting hot under the collar.
- My feathers have been ruffled!
- A storm is brewing.
- Signing a time-out by making a "T" with both hands.

However you communicate your need for a time-out (humor can help), the key is to verbalize in some way that you care about each other and that you will work it out later. Communicate that your buttons have been pushed and that you are no longer safe in the conversation, but you will return and resolve the issue at a later time. How will you communicate that you need a time-out in your own words?

The other objection that I hear when encouraging people to take a time-out is the "Don't let the sun go down on your anger" argument. Most of us are familiar with this passage of Scripture: "In your anger do not sin: Do not let the sun go down while you are still angry, and do not give the devil a foothold" (Ephesians 4:26–27). Many well-meaning Christian couples have interpreted these verses to mean that we must not go to bed until we've resolved our conflict. I used to keep Erin up until the wee hours of the morning in a futile attempt to keep the sun from going down on our conflict. Does keeping my wife up past our bedtime in the attempt to resolve an argument actually work? No! Seriously, when was the last time you had a productive, honoring discussion in the middle of the night? This verse is saying don't let the sun go down on your *anger*. It doesn't say don't let the sun go down on your conflict *issues*. That is a huge difference. The reason not to go to bed angry has more to do with the state of your heart than it does with whatever you were fighting about. When you go to sleep with a closed heart, you are extremely susceptible to Satan's attacks.

As a quick review, here is the process of hitting the pause button, or calling a time-out:

- Interrupt the conflict by expressing your need to hit the pause button.
- Communicate your love and desire to solve the problem together at a later time, when your heart is open. Try to confirm a time to resume the discussion.
- Give each other space to calm down (a twenty-minute break).
- Get your heart open, gain perspective, and think clearly.

Now that you've interrupted the Reactive Cycle, watch how powerful step two is.

2. Identify Your Emotions

Now that you have hit the pause button and created some emotional space, the question, is what do you do in your time-out? Many people continue to think about their spouse and what he or she did that was so offensive or hurtful. However, if you continue to focus on these things, you will stay upset and likely stay in reaction mode. Instead, the key is to transition into thinking about your emotions.

"Be quick to listen, slow to speak and slow to anger" (James 1:19). This powerful counsel is usually applied to relationships. We should be quick to listen to others, especially our spouse. But I want to encourage you to look at this verse from a different angle. When your buttons get pushed, you need to be quick to listen to *you*. That sounds selfish? Here's the reality. When you go into reaction mode, you are no longer safe. There is no way you can listen to your spouse when you react, because your heart is closed. I don't care how relationally savvy you are, when your buttons have been pushed, you cannot "be quick to listen" until you calm down, deescalate your emotions, and get your heart back open. The best listening is done from the heart. It's called empathy. And empathy requires an open heart.

When you get away from your spouse to calm down, the next step is to identify your buttons—your emotions. Just like creating space was key for the fighters, this step is vital for the "flighters," because they tend to ignore their emotions. Instead, welcome your feelings! Rather than denying they exist, ignoring them, stuffing them away, or minimizing their importance, honor them. I recently read a great quote: "Emotions are celebrated and repressed, analyzed and medicated, adored and ignored—but rarely, if ever, are they honored."[7]

We honor our emotions when we identify them—put a name to how we are feeling. This has a powerful effect. Actually, one study discovered that when you name a specific feeling, it reduces the intensity of that emotion. Brain scans show that putting heightened emotions into words calms the brain's emotion center (remember the amygdala). By naming your emotions, you are able to put a label on your feelings, which is the first step in dealing with them in an appropriate manner.[8] I think this is why King David wrote, "In your anger do not sin; when you are on your beds, search your hearts and be silent" (Psalm 4:4). Be silent and search your heart. And since emotions are the voice of your heart, searching your heart includes identifying specific feelings.

When an argument flares up, the wise man quenches it with silence.

—AUTHOR UNKNOWN

This can be challenging for many people. Listen to how one husband described his frustration around identifying his emotions.

I've been told that naming emotions is important, but I'm terrible at doing this. In reality, I have managed to successfully turn off a lot of my emotions. This has been the case for several years. Now, if something starts to get too emotional, I normally just get a really bad headache and avoid the issue. I have realized that my coping method is not helping my marriage. Lately, I have been trying to focus more on my emotions, and I realize that I typically just have this jumble of emotions that includes everything from anger to guilt to sadness to whatever. They are all mixed together and inseparable.[9]

How do you separate your emotions and name your feelings? The best place to start is with the buttons that you checked on the chart in Chapter 2. You can also pinpoint your feelings by asking yourself some important questions:

What am I feeling right now?

What are my specific buttons that just got pushed?

Where is this feeling coming from?

What is it saying about me?

What message or lie about me am I buying into right now?

The key is to treat your feelings as information. Don't judge, stifle, minimize, or ignore your emotions; instead, view them as valuable information. The real worth and value of our emotions is that they are a great source of data. However, most people make the mistake of viewing emotions as positive or negative and good or bad. They mistakenly believe that they need to get rid of negative or bad feelings. Once again, that has the mark of the enemy all over it! He wants us to view our feelings as negative so that we stay oblivious to our emotions. We then miss out on some important information. The truth is that our emotions are incredibly valuable because they are messengers—they deliver important information about our individual needs, desires, hopes, and fears. Our emotions can teach us about our relationships if we take the time to listen. Just as yawning tells us we need to sleep, our emotions warn us about possible dangers and potential opportunities. The key is to be curious about your feelings; allow them to have space to breathe and come to the surface. This is why I love the quote by Robyn Posin, "The thing to do with feelings is to make it safe to feel all of them!" Once you identify your feelings, don't try to figure out what to do with them. Don't try to fix how you feel. Instead, take a step further and ask yourself, "What are my emotions trying to tell me?" What could it mean, for example, if you are feeling stressed out, worried, sad, fearful, hurt, or frustrated?

Sitting in our SUV, I didn't want to think about my feelings. I wanted to dwell on how Erin wounded me or what I should have said to the biker. However, I finally forced myself to decide what buttons had been pushed. For me, it was my "failure" button and "making a mistake" button. My mistake had cost my family money that we didn't really have. As a matter of fact, the money that it would cost to repair the man's motorcycle would have to come from our vacation money. Talk about feeling like a failure! I also felt humiliated by the man's tirade and disrespected as he cursed at me. When I got back in our vehicle, these buttons were so stirred up that it took only one comment from Erin to reignite them. When Erin "lovingly" encouraged me to pay closer attention pulling out, I felt controlled and criticized. Needless to say, there was a lot going on for me internally. In the past, I wouldn't have paid attention to my feelings. Putting a name to these buttons did help me calm down as I drove toward the airport. More important, accurately identifying my feelings allowed me to take the final and most powerful step in the process.

3. Discover God's Truth About Your Emotions

Once you better understand which buttons were pushed, don't stop there. Determine the truth about your emotions. In spite of what our culture wants us to believe, we are not the source of truth. Our feelings are a valuable source of information, but that doesn't mean we accept our emotions as truth. Just because we feel something doesn't mean we act upon it. This would make us just as dangerous as the person who doesn't feel at all.

Remember, when we are in reaction mode (fight or flight) and our heart is closed, it can be difficult to gain any kind of insight or understand the truth. Don't forget that Satan tries hard to deceive you. He wants to write lies on your heart and lie to you about your spouse and marriage. You fight back when you remember that your feelings don't necessarily equal facts. Simply because you think or feel something doesn't automatically make it the truth. And just because another person thinks or feels something doesn't mean that it's true about you.

Don't let Satan, you, or others be your source of truth! Instead, ask God to reveal His truth. "But when he, the Spirit of truth, comes, he will guide you into all truth" (John 16:13). Specifically, ask God to reveal His perspective and what is true about you—your feelings, thoughts, and situation. "The unfolding of your words gives light; it gives understanding" (Psalm 119:130). You are asking for His insight—His truth. Pray these questions from your heart and not from your brain:

What is the truth about my emotions?

What is the truth about me?

Is what my wife/husband is saying about me true?

What lie is Satan trying to write on my heart?

What do I need to take responsibility for?

Who is the person I want to be in this moment—the person God created me to be?

Look at how I was attacked on the way to the airport. I felt like a failure when I knocked over the motorcycle. I felt humiliated and disrespected when the biker yelled and swore at me. I felt controlled as Erin tried to help me navigate out of the gas station. What was the truth? I wish I had known to immediately go to my heavenly Father and ask if the truth was that I was a failure for hitting the man's bike. I didn't know how to do this step. I could have asked God what was true about the people who had observed the altercation. How did they see me? My fear was that they didn't respect me. Was that an accurate reading according to my heavenly Father? What about my wife? Was she trying to control me by telling me how to drive? God knows her heart. We cannot rely on our own perception, interpretation, insight, discernment, observation, opinion, or analysis. We are human and will often miss the truth about our emotions or the motives of our spouse. This is exactly why King Solomon advised, "Trust in the LORD with all your heart and lean not on your own understanding" (Proverbs 3:5). We become unsafe when we lean on our own understanding and blindly accept or act upon our emotions or thoughts.

To become acquainted with oneself is a terrible shock.

—CARL JUNG

Let me say this even stronger: You have no business confronting your spouse about anything until you've first prayed about it. It's imperative that we seek God's perspective and gain his insight before we talk to our spouse. When you get hurt, you have your own issues entangled in your hurt. You cannot simply make your pain 100 percent your spouse's fault. Your spouse's behavior will push your buttons, but so does your own stuff. In other words, when your buttons get pushed, there are always two guilty parties:

What your spouse did—his or her hurtful words or actions

What you bring to the table—your expectations, past experiences, family upbringing, fears, pet peeves; feeling tired, exhausted, hungry, sick, etc.

Before you exclusively focus on your spouse's side and what he or she did, *first* take a look at your side. Your spouse might do something that pushes one of your buttons. However, that doesn't mean it was totally his or her fault—it may not be at all. The truth might be that you're hypersensitive to a certain word or phrase or tone of voice that your father used when you were young. And now, when your spouse says it, it's like fingernails on a chalkboard. It's not wrong for your spouse to use that word or tone of voice; that's your stuff. Your spouse might do something that is hurtful, but the intensity of your pain might have more to do with your issues than with what he or she actually did. You need to own what you bring to the Reactive Cycle before you make your spouse the problem. The point is, before you go charging off to confront your spouse, or before you shut down, ask the Lord to help you separate your stuff from your spouse's stuff. Pray for God's wisdom and insight into your issues. You become a safe person when you are able to parcel out your issues that have nothing to do with your spouse, then you can identify your spouse's issues (what your spouse did that was hurtful).

This is what I do now when people share negative things about me—especially my wife. In the past, when Erin shared how I'd hurt her, disappointed her, frustrated her, wounded her, or made her feel unsafe, I would defend myself or debate her feelings or interpretations. Now I do my best to take her words to the Lord. For example, I'll say to Erin, "If I'm hearing you right, you believe that I don't value you and that you're not important or a priority to me. Let me pray about what you're sharing, and I'll come to you when I've heard from the Lord." I really do pray about what Erin shared; it isn't some creative new way to get out of listening to my wife, although I'm certain that she was suspicious in the beginning. I've been doing it for years now, and Erin trusts that when I say I'm going to pray about what she has shared, I'm going to pray. I wish I could tell you that I do it perfectly, but I'd be lying. Many times I initially argue, debate, and defend myself when she shares her feelings or her opinions about me. However, I eventually go to the Lord in prayer about what Erin (or anyone) is saying about me. I don't allow people to be the source of truth in my life. I absolutely believe that God can and does use others to speak truth into my life: "As iron sharpens iron, so one man sharpens another" (Proverbs 27:17). It's difficult, when someone is sharing hurt or frustration, to know what is truth versus what are personal issues. Many times the truth gets entangled with his or her stuff. God is the only one who can unravel that emotional mess and sort out the truth. This is what Acts 17:11 encouraged as well: "For they received the message with great eagerness and examined the Scriptures every day to see if what Paul said was true." We need God's help when examining our own feelings or what people say about us in order to understand the truth.

When I pray about how Erin is feeling or what she has said about me, nine times out of ten, the Lord confirms what Erin was saying. It's humbling and convicting. This is why I love Philippians 4:7: "And the peace of God, which transcends all understanding, will guard your hearts and your minds in Christ Jesus." It's the only other place in the entire Bible (besides Proverbs 4:23) where God uses the phrase "guard your heart." When we pray to the Lord, He gives us peace that surpasses all human understanding. It's God's truth that ends up guarding our heart and mind. It's not my wife's job to convict me or be my source of truth. She doesn't want that job, anyway. That's God's job, and He does an amazing job if we open our heart and mind to His loving correction. "Blessed are those whom God corrects; so do not despise the discipline of the Almighty" (Job 5:17). This is true because "the Lord disciplines those he loves" (Hebrews 12:6).

I've learned that you cannot make someone love you; all you can do is be someone who can be loved.

—ANONYMOUS

As we seek His truth, God will help us see things through His eyes: "This then is how we know that we belong to the truth, and how we set our hearts at rest in his presence whenever our hearts condemn us, for God is greater than our hearts and he knows everything" (1 John 3:19–20). As we gain his perspective, we will see the truth, and it will open our heart. "Then you will know the truth, and the truth will set you free" (John 8:32). This is what I want: a heart that has been set free and is now open.

It's been my experience that taking a time-out and identifying your emotions will calm you down, but seeking God's truth is really the step that opens your heart. And once your heart is open and full of love, you are ready to respond (rather than react) to your spouse.

Eight

Unlocking Healthy Conflict

There are few things in life as disheartening as unhealthy conflict. When couples are entrenched in the Reactive Cycle, it's extremely difficult to see past the hurt and frustration. It's like the insurance salesman who explained to his customer, "You've filled in this application all right except for one thing, Mr. Perkins. Where it asks the relationship of Mrs. Perkins to yourself, you should have put down 'wife,' not 'strained.'"

A strained marriage is often riddled with unhealthy conflict and closed hearts. Over time, that can lead to hardened hearts. But it doesn't have to be this way; conflict doesn't have to destroy relationships. The truth is that conflict has the ability to strengthen marriage relationships. As I've said, healthy conflict is a doorway to intimacy. It can facilitate deeper communication, understanding, trust, connection, and respect—true intimacy—if we choose to manage differences and arguments in nourishing ways. Healthy conflict is the entryway to discovering our spouse's most important feelings and needs. It's like my good friend Gary J. Oliver says: "The more we try to deny, hide from, overlook, and otherwise avoid conflict, the greater the problem becomes. It is how we choose to respond to conflict that produces the growth or creates the real problem."[1] Thus, tapping into the power of healthy conflict is a matter of opening the door, not closing it.

So, how do we open the door? We need a key. And the key to unlocking the door of healthy conflict is *safety*.

THE KEY TO HEALTHY CONFLICT

When Jesus talked about divorce in the context of a hardened heart, He also explained that it wasn't God's original plan. Jesus said, "Moses permitted you to divorce your wives because your hearts were hard. But it was not this way from the beginning" (Matthew 19:8). His last statement suggests that God's perfect plan for marriage is the opposite of hardheartedness: two open hearts. This is why the strategy for breaking the Reactive Cycle is to get both hearts open. We dealt with your heart in the last chapter. Let's do a quick review.

Jesus explained how to stop unhealthy conflict and how to get your heart open when He encouraged us to get the log out of our own eye before worrying about the speck of sawdust in our spouse's eye. Instead of avoiding conflict or trying to change your spouse, deal with you and get your heart back open, so that instead of reacting you can respond to your spouse. It's impossible to have a productive conflict discussion when your heart is closed. Reacting is always a sign of a closed heart; on the other hand, responding is evidence of an open heart. When our heart is open, God's love is flowing through us. This is why King Solomon passionately encouraged us to "guard our heart," because it is the wellspring of life (Proverbs

4:23). When and only when God's love is flowing out from our open heart are we capable of being patient, kind, gentle, generous, humble, honoring, peaceful, forgiving, and so on (1 Corinthians 13:4–5)—the exact characteristics needed for healthy conflict and to get to the deepest levels of intimacy.

A joyful heart is the inevitable result of a heart burning with love.

—MOTHER TERESA

I love the saying, "Wherever you go, go with all your heart." That sounds similar to the Greatest Commandment, doesn't it? "Love the Lord your God with all your heart." When your heart is open, you are safe to respond to your spouse. But in order to have a great conversation in a way that helps break the Reactive Cycle, your spouse's heart needs to be open as well. This can be challenging. Your spouse, like many of us, may struggle to keep his or her heart open, because openness can make people feel vulnerable. As Arch Hart and Sharon Hart Morris explain:

> When a husband and wife love each other, they literally give their hearts to each other for safekeeping. This is such a delicate, trusting act that any violation or injury of this trust can cause the most painful of reactions. Imagine taking the very essence of your being—your heart—and placing it in the hands of your spouse. Your heart becomes your mate's to care for, safeguard, cherish, and love. This necessitates a willingness to be vulnerable and take a bold, risky step. If your partner re-

ciprocates, you both have chosen to risk being hurt, rejected, and abandoned. Placing your heart in the hands of another is a giant step of faith. Afterward, you can only wait to see what your spouse will do with your heart. Your desire, of course, is that your spouse will be a safe haven for your heart. And that is your spouse's longing as well.[2]

Love is risky. There is no guarantee that we won't get hurt. We feel vulnerable because we can't control what our spouse will ultimately say or do once we grant access to our heart. There will always be a chance of getting hurt—rejected, devalued, unappreciated, controlled, unloved, or disrespected.

How do we create a deep connection with our spouse in spite of the obvious risks? It's important to create the right type of environment for our spouse's heart to open. In other words, to get from unhealthy conflict to the deepest levels of intimacy, you must create an atmosphere of safety. Let me explain what I mean by sharing a story about some good friends of mine who were looking to buy their first home. One day Jackson and Krista's (not their real names) Realtor showed them a charming turn-of-the-century home. Krista instantly fell in love.

"It's close to town and a great park," she happily explained to Jackson. "We could restore it and make some money if we ever wanted to sell. But why would we ever want to leave such an amazing place? We could raise our kids here and grow old playing with our grandkids at the park!" That was how Krista described the "mature" house. Jackson, on the other hand, calmly described it as "a ton of work!"

I guess it's all just a matter of perspective.

As a young married couple, they could afford the house only by recruiting Jackson's dad and builder friend John to do most of the work. They would have to renovate the kitchen, build a new bathroom, get a new roof, and paint the entire inside and outside.

Love is the enchanted dawn of every heart.

—ALPHONSE DE LAMARTINE

In spite of the overwhelming punch list of items to be fixed, Krista, the eternal optimist, was certain the house would be ready in one month. Regardless of any unrealistic expectations, she began to plan a huge housewarming party.

Starting the projects required Jackson to make calls to his dad, to John, and to the various subcontractors. However, Jackson was busy starting a new job at a family ministry, and he hadn't made a single phone call.

"What did your dad say?" Krista asked each day. "When can John start building the bathroom? Have you hired a roofer?" She was anxious to get the projects going because the party date was coming up fast.

Jackson's standard response was always "No, but I will."

You could feel the tension mounting between them like a volcano.

As part of Jackson's new job, his boss wanted him to attend a training seminar on a technique for ministering to married couples. (I'm not making this up!) As an added bonus, Jackson was able to take Krista on this all-expenses-paid trip.

The relational volcano erupted on day two of the marriage conference.

"Have you called your dad yet?" Krista implored.

"No," answered Jackson, irritated, "but I will."

"You keep saying that you will," snapped Krista, "but you haven't. We need to make the plans now, before these people get too busy!"

"Get off my back," Jackson reacted defensively. "We're in Dallas. It's not like I can start the work tomorrow. I'll call when we get home."

"What's going on?" Krista asked in disbelief. "Why aren't you calling anyone?"

"I've got plenty of time," Jackson shot back. "We can't even move into the house for another month. What's the big deal? Besides, I haven't had time, what with my new job and attending this conference."

"Fine!" Krista declared, throwing her hands up in the air. "I'll make the calls."

They spent the rest of the day in stony silence.

On the last day of the training conference, the instructor asked for a volunteer couple who'd be willing to share a recent conflict that the group could help them resolve using their newly acquired skills.

It is only with the heart that one can see rightly; what is essential is invisible to the eye.

—ANTOINE DE SAINT-EXUPÉRY

Jackson tried his best to disappear into the crowd, but all of a sudden, out of the corner of his eye, he noticed Krista waving her hand in the air. "Who is she waving at?" thought Jackson. And then it hit him. His wife was volunteering them!

It was like one of those slow-motion movie scenes, where Jackson is screaming, "Noooooo!" and reaching for her hand to pull it down before anyone notices.

Too late!

"Excellent," the instructor said as she happily clapped her hands together. "Let's give this brave couple a hand as they come up."

Glaring at Krista, Jackson sat in one of the two chairs positioned in front of the group of enthusiastic students. As if to add insult to injury, they had to sit knee to knee and hold hands. I'm certain Jackson had zero desire to touch his wife's knee, hold her hand, or gaze deeply into her eyes.

The last thing Jackson heard before this nightmare unfolded was the group leader saying, "Resolving conflict is just like remodeling a house . . ." I'll finish Jackson and Krista's story in a moment, but first I want to make a very important point about emotional safety.

I'm going out on a limb, but I'm guessing that discussing their disagreement in front of a group of total strangers didn't make Jackson feel very safe. Likewise, there are plenty of ways in which we make our spouse feel unsafe when trying to work through conflict. Think back to the list of reactions that we use when our buttons get pushed. For example:

- Criticism
- Withdrawal
- Escalation
- Negative beliefs
- Sarcasm
- Stuffing down our feelings
- Defensiveness
- Judgment
- Anger

These reactions and many others make a relationship feel unsafe. Hearts shut down, Satan attacks our minds, and we disconnect from each other. And yet if we want to successfully manage our disagreements, we need to focus on creating the right type of atmosphere or environment. The key is to foster safety—a marriage that feels like the safest place on earth.

My heart is ever at your service.

—WILLIAM SHAKESPEARE

CREATE A SAFE MARRIAGE

The best approach to foster intimacy and deep connection after the Reactive Cycle is to focus time, attention, and energy on creating relational space that feels safe. When your spouse feels safe, he is naturally inclined to relax and open his heart. In this peaceful state, openness simply happens. It occurs effortlessly and doesn't require conscious thought. You don't have to force intimacy or do things to create connection when you feel safe. Intimacy just happens when you feel safe with a person. This is true because God designed our heart to be open. Literally, the default setting of a heart is openness. It takes much more effort and energy to stay closed and shut down than to stay open. Think about a recent time when your spouse hurt or frustrated you. Remember how quickly your heart shut down? Once your heart closed, you instantly reacted in some way (fight or flight) and ultimately disconnected. By now you know the cycle! But your heart was not designed to stay closed. Maintaining a closed heart is like trying to force a huge beach ball underwater. You have to strain and push to keep a ball full of air underwater. It's the same with your heart. You have to work really hard to keep a heart full of God's love shut down. Have you ever noticed, when your spouse takes responsibility for her actions and seeks forgiveness, how quickly your heart opens back up? Like that beach ball under the water, once you feel safe, your heart will explode back open. You can go from feeling shut down to instantly feeling connected and open.

Emotional safety sets a peaceful environment that allows people to relax. This is why, in your quest for reconnection after the Reactive Cycle, I want to encourage you to make creating safety a top priority. Hopefully, you now see that the only way to become one is to intertwine two open hearts together. I like what two Christian authors say about creating a safe marriage:

> Marriage is the sanctuary of the heart. You have been entrusted with the heart of another human being. Whatever else your life's great mission will entail, loving and defending this heart next to you is part of your great quest. Marriage is the privilege and the honor of living as close to the heart as two people can get. No one else in all the world has the opportunity to know each other more intimately than do a husband and wife. We are invited into their secret lives, their truest selves; we come to know their nuances, their particular tastes, what they think is funny, what drives them crazy. We are entrusted with their hopes and dreams, their wounds, and their fears.[3]

I couldn't agree more. In a marriage, we get the privilege of being invited into the "holy of holies"—our spouse's heart. In the same way that the Israelites treated this special place in their temple with the utmost respect (the high priest had to be completely purified, or he would die), we must treat our spouse's heart—her deepest feelings, desires, hopes, and fears—with care and respect. Only then will we be given access to her holy of holies. How do we pull this off? How do we create a marriage that feels like the safest place on earth? The process begins by clearly understanding what a safe marriages looks like.

The greatest gift that you can give to others is the gift of unconditional love and acceptance.

—BRIAN TRACY

WHAT IS EMOTIONAL SAFETY?

Most marriage books focus on some new research or counseling technique or teach you the latest five principles or hottest seven steps. But the newest skills won't give you what you really want: to feel loved, close, valued, respected, cherished, and deeply connected.

A heart will open only when it feels safe! I've learned the hard way that there isn't a single skill or tool I could offer that will make any difference if hearts are shut down. That is how I hope this book is different from others you might read. I won't attempt to teach you communication skills or tools to problem solve until the proper foundation of emotional safety is set—knowing that if both hearts aren't open, true intimacy and deep connection isn't possible.

To experience true intimacy requires that you feel safe with each other. But what does feeling safe really mean? I asked more than a thousand couples for help defining emotional safety. Listen to some of their answers:

- Feeling completely secure
- Being accepted for who I am
- Feeling relaxed and comfortable
- Being free to express who I really am
- Being loved unconditionally
- Feeling respected
- Knowing that my spouse is trustworthy
- Having my spouse be there for me
- Being fully understood
- Being valued and honored
- Having loving reassurance
- Being able to open fully in order to give and receive love
- Not being judged
- Being seen for who I am (*"into me see"*)
- Having my flaws accepted as part of the whole package
- Living in an atmosphere of open communication

Wouldn't it be amazing for these things to be the foundation of marriage? Feeling emotionally safe is critical for a marriage to thrive. Here's how author Barbara DeAngelis explains the importance of creating safety.

One of our most basic needs . . . in an intimate relationship is the need to feel safe. I'm not talking about physical safety, but rather the feeling of emotional safety. It is the deep sense that the relationship is solid, that our partner's affections are serious and committed, that we can trust the love we feel, and thus allow ourselves to open fully to give and receive it. This emotional safety is the key that unlocks a person's heart and soul. When we feel safe, we are able to open up. When we feel safe, we are able to risk. When we feel safe, we are able to relax. When we feel safe, we are able to shine.[4]

I define emotional safety as feeling free to open up and reveal who you really are while trusting that the other person will still love, value, and unconditionally accept you. In other words, you feel safe with someone when you are confident and trust that he or she will handle your heart—your deepest feelings, thoughts, desires, hopes, and dreams—with the utmost care. Most people long to offer their heart to another person and say, "Here I am; the true me. This is me spiritually, emotionally, physically, and mentally. I want you to know the depths of my heart and see into the very bowels of my soul. I want you to appreciate who I am in the deepest rooms of my heart—places that I let only the most trustworthy of people visit. Be careful and patient with me; I am a valuable person who will take more than one lifetime to truly get to know!"

Dinah Craik explains emotional safety this way:

Oh, the comfort—the inexpressible comfort of feeling safe with a person—having neither to weigh thoughts nor measure words, but pouring them all right out, just as they are . . . certain that a faithful hand will take and sift them, keep what is worth keeping, and then with the breath of kindness blow the rest away.[5]

What I love about this quote is that it was written in 1859. Emotional safety is as true now as it was back in the mid-1800s. So, how do we build a marriage that feels like the safest place on earth?

To stay in love, live from your heart.

—TUPELO KENYON

CREATING SAFETY FOR OPEN HEARTS

Emotional safety is not simply a bunch of psychobabble. Safety is, first and foremost, something that our heavenly Father provides for us.

- The name of the LORD is a strong tower; the righteous run to it and are safe. (Proverbs 18:10)
- Keep me safe, O God, for in you I take refuge. (Psalm 16:1)
- In peace I will lie down and sleep, for you alone, LORD, make me dwell in safety. (Psalm 4:8)
- Fear of man will prove to be a snare, but whoever trusts in the LORD is kept safe. (Proverbs 29:25)
- The Lord will rescue me from every evil attack and will bring me safely to his heavenly kingdom. (2 Timothy 4:18)

These are just a few of the many verses that show how the God of this universe goes out of His way to make us feel safe. He wants our heart open so he can love through us. And hearts open when they feel safe. The safest relationship we will ever have is with our heavenly Father. I want to model my earthly relationships after what God does with me. The key to creating a marriage that feels like the safest place on earth is found in Ephesians 5:29: "For no one ever hated his own flesh, but nourishes and cherishes it, just as Christ also does the church." Creating a safe marriage involves both an attitude and an action. *Cherish* is the right attitude, and *nourish* is the powerful action. Let's look first at the attitude that we need in order to foster safety in our marriage.

1. CHERISH:
Recognize Your Spouse's Incredible Value

The primary attitude that will help your spouse feel emotionally safe is when he believes that you understand how incredibly valuable he is. That is the essence of honor. The literal definition of honor is "to give preference to someone by attaching high value to them."[6] Honor is a decision to view our spouse as a priceless treasure—a person of high worth and value. This is what King Solomon encouraged as well: "A man's greatest treasure is his wife" (Proverbs 18:22). Honor isn't based on behavior or subject to emotion. You grant your spouse value whether or not they want it or deserve it. Honor is a decision you make and a gift you give. This is exactly what the apostle Paul encouraged the early Christians to do when he wrote, "Be devoted to one another in brotherly love; give preference to one another in honor" (Romans 12:10). What great marriage advice! However, we don't have to rely on our own observations to attach value to our spouse. God has made it resplendently clear that my wife is valuable. Look at some of these great verses that show how much our heavenly Father values and cherishes us:

- "For you were made in my image." Genesis 1:27
- "I chose you when I planned creation." Ephesians 1:11–12
- "You are fearfully and wonderfully made." Psalm 139:14
- "For you are my treasured possession." Exodus 19:5
- "You are my glorious inheritance." Ephesians 1:18

It's amazing to think that the God of this universe considers my wife His treasured possession and that Jesus says that she is His glorious inheritance. That's powerful! However, when Erin and I are in the midst of the Reactive Cycle and my heart closes, the first thing to go is my awareness of her incredible value. And in those moments, when I fail to see her as my heavenly Father sees His daughter, I'm not safe. When I lose sight of her value, when I'm not cherishing her, I'm more apt to react and treat her in dishonoring ways. Then Erin has every right to put up a wall and protect herself.

Being able to share yourself in an atmosphere of safety and trust is the key to overcoming the fear that inhibits love.

—HAROLD H. BLOOMFIELD

Honoring or cherishing your spouse is the attitude that creates a safe marriage. Marriage expert John Gottman says that "without honor, all the marriage skills one can learn won't work."[7] Expert Scott Stanley says that "honor is the fuel that keeps the lifelong marriage loving and functioning. If only a spark of respect or adoration remains, the spark can be turned into the flame in a few days."[8]

I watched the power of recognizing my wife's value this past Thanksgiving. My family spent the holiday weekend at my parents' home in Branson, Missouri. One of the things that I appreciate most about my parents is the honesty of their marriage. They've never claimed to have a "perfect" marriage and aren't afraid to disagree.

At one point, my parents got into a huge argument. I couldn't even tell you what it was about (I'm sure they don't remember, either!). The funny part was watching a couple who have been married over forty-eight years still getting upset with each other.

They were so frustrated that they each ran off to a different part of the house. Of course, all of the women chased after my mother to provide emotional comfort and support. Since I was the only guy present, I figured I'd better chase after my father. But instead of providing empathy or emotional support, I reasoned that my dad needed to laugh.

As I trailed after my father, heading for his home office, I suggested what I thought was a very good idea. "Hey, Dad," I said laughing, "since you've written like fifty marriage books, how about if I pull one off the shelf and read what you should be doing for Mom right now?"

I thought my banter was quite funny.

His office door slamming in my face indicated that he disagreed with me.

I let the situation calm down for a few minutes before I knocked on his door.

"Come in," he reluctantly replied.

As I walked into his office, I found my dad sitting behind his computer. I wasn't sure what he was doing, but I assumed he was online reading the news or looking at the weather. When I walked up behind him, I was surprised by what he was looking at.

I found him reading a document entitled "Why Norma Is So Valuable." (My mom's name is Norma, just in case you were wondering.)

"What are you reading?" I asked.

"Well," my dad began, "a number of years ago I started a list of why your mom is so valuable. So when I'm upset with her, or when we've had a fight, I've learned that instead of sitting here thinking about how hurt or frustrated I am at your mother, I need to make myself read through this list."

The best and most beautiful things in the world cannot be seen or even touched. They must be felt with the heart.

—HELEN KELLER

The document contained literally hundreds of words and phrases describing my mom's value. It was amazing.

"When I first start to read through the list, I'm still upset," explained my dad. "I usually get to the first three or four items and think, 'What was I thinking?' or 'This one is no longer valid!' or 'I'm definitely going to erase that one.' But then the farther down I read, the faster I realize that you have an amazing mom."

This is the best idea I've ever heard for recognizing someone's value. Talk about creating safety. It's also what my father does to get his heart back open. Luke 12:34 explains why it is so powerful: "For where your treasure is, so there will your heart be also." In other words, your heart will be open to what you value. One way to keep your heart open and your spouse feeling safe with you is to focus on her value.

The great news is that we can create this honor list for our spouse as well. Take several minutes to complete the following exercise.

In the space on page 168, list all the reasons why your spouse is so valuable. For example: a character trait, gender difference, faith pattern, values, morals, parenting skills, spirituality, the roles s/he plays that you appreciate (i.e., worker, friend, parent, sibling, son), personality characteristic, how s/he treats you, etc.

Here are some words to prime the pump and get you thinking about your spouse's value:

Humble	Respectful	Responsible	Curious
Brave	Considerate	Helpful	Determined
Integrity	Creative	Dreamer	Energetic
Courageous	Independent	Happy	Cheerful
Funny	Intelligent	Leader	Thoughtful
Loyal	Honest	Gentle	Calm
Caring	Adventurous	Loving	Mannerly
Unselfish	Hard-working	Neat	
Generous	Fun-loving	Joyful	
Self-confident	Successful	Cooperative	

Be sure to keep the list nearby so you can periodically add to it and revise it when you need to remember your spouse's value. Also, don't keep the amazing list to yourself—share it with your spouse. Let her know that you recognize her value. When this happens, not only does your spouse benefit, but you are positively impacted as well.

As wonderful as it is to cherish your spouse's incredible worth, attitude without action is meaningless. James wrote, "Do not merely listen to the word, and so deceive yourselves. Do what it says" (James 1:22). Once you recognize your spouse's value, back up that attitude with action.

2. Nourish: Treat Your Spouse in Valuable Ways

Understanding your spouse's incredible value is the beginning of safety, but to create a marriage that feels like the safest place on earth, you must be able to express honor through action and behavior. "Let us not love with mere words or tongue but with actions and in truth" (1 John 3:18). Honor in action means that you learn how to handle your spouse's heart—her deepest feelings, thoughts, and desires—with the utmost care. You need to visualize his heart tattooed with the words "Handle with care."

Let's quickly review the definition of "emotional safety": feeling free to open up and reveal who you really are and trust that the other person will still love, value, and accept you. As you can see, the last part of the definition communicates a powerful message: "You are incredibly valuable, so don't be afraid of letting me see your heart. You can share your deepest feelings, thoughts, opinions, hopes, dreams, fears, hurts, and memories, and I will still love and accept you." Safety in action means that you handle your spouse's heart in extremely careful and honoring ways.

Let me make practical the idea of safety in action. If you want to treat your spouse in valuable ways, you need to focus on caring. One of my favorite quotes is by former president Theodore Roosevelt: "People don't care how much you know until he knows how much you care." Isn't that a powerful relationship principle? Your spouse isn't going to care about your knowledge, insights, wisdom, or solutions until he knows that you care.

Remember Jackson and Krista from earlier in the chapter? We left Jackson sitting in front of a group of strangers at a marriage-training seminar, about to discuss a big fight around the remodeling of their home. How in the world can they have a meaningful conversation and get to the deepest levels of intimacy and connection? Never underestimate the power of caring.

In this moment, Jackson didn't care what Krista knew or what was going on with her. His heart was closed; he didn't feel safe. But instead of trying to get Jackson to care about her pain and frustration, Krista made it her goal to care about Jackson's heart.

"I so greatly appreciate your sense of responsibility, and the fact that when you say you're going to do something, it will always happen," Krista started. "You are such a man of integrity. I think this is why I've been confused about the lack of follow-through around this remodel. Would you be willing to help me understand what is going on for you?"

When you choose to care for your spouse, it can instantly create a safe environment to share your deepest thoughts and feelings.

"You're right," Jackson cautiously responded with fifty sets of ears trained on his every word. "I'm usually great at follow-through. But this project has made me realize just how inadequate I am around home repair. My dad is so great at it. As a builder, John is amazing. I think I realized that I couldn't do anything without their help. That made me feel like a failure. Since this is our first house, I want to feel competent. I want you to trust that if something breaks, I can fix it without having to call my dad or some repairman."

Krista instantly held Jackson's hand tight in her own and, with big tears in her eyes, smiled at her husband. "That makes so much sense," she said gently. "I had no idea that you felt this way. I am so sorry that you have been feeling like a failure."

As twenty-five women collectively exhaled, "Ahhhhh," two hearts were reconnected.

This is the power of safety in action. Caring has the power to soften a closed heart. Sara Paddison, in her book *The Hidden Power of the Heart,* says, "Care is the ingredient that keeps true friendships alive despite separation, distance, or time. Care gives latitude to another person and gets you past the dislikes and annoyances. Quite simply, caring sustains love."[9] This is exactly what the apostle Peter was trying to convey when he wrote, "Love each other deeply from the heart" (1 Peter 1:22). Your spouse will feel emotionally cared for when you attend to her heart.

Compassion is the most important emotion in marriage and intimate relationships, contributing far more to happiness than love does. Relationships can be happy with low levels of love and high levels of compassion, but not the other way around.

—STEVEN STOSNY

The key to put caring into action is compassion. This is exactly what Krista did for Jackson. King Solomon said it best: "Words from a wise man's mouth are gracious" (Ecclesiastes 10:12). Another word for "gracious" as it's used here is "compassionate." The verse could also read, "Words from a wise man's mouth are compassionate." According to the Psychology Wiki online encyclopedia, compassion is defined as a "profound human emotion prompted by the pain of others. More vigorous than empathy, the feeling commonly gives rise to an active desire to alleviate another's suffering."[10]

Certainly, compassion is an important first step to move from unhealthy conflict into intimacy. Just ask Jackson. Allow your spouse's pain that was caused by the Reactive Cycle to drive you to a place of compassion. When you come together to talk, make your first goal to alleviate their hurt and emotional pain. I love what marriage expert Steven Stosny concluded about the importance of compassion:

> Most marriages end in a whimper, not a bang. The final rupture is not caused by too much anger or abuse or infidelity. Rather, most marriages die a slow, agonizing death from too little compassion. Compassion is sympathy for the hurt or distress of another. At the heart, it is a simple appreciation of the basic human frailty we all share, which is why the experience of compassion makes you feel more humane and less isolated. . . . Most of what you fight about now is not money or sex or in-laws or raising the kids. Those are common problems that seem insurmountable only when you're hurt. What causes the hurt, i.e., what you really fight about, is the impression that your partner doesn't care how you feel.[11]

Read his last sentence again: "What causes the hurt, i.e., what you really fight about, is the impression that your partner doesn't care how you feel." That's right! Our unhealthy conflict comes from those deeper heart issues. Here is where compassion can help. When we come together to talk about the conflict, we can use compassion to help our spouse feel cared for. This instantly creates safety.

A heart will open when it feels safe. If you tried to pry open a roly-poly bug curled up in a tight little ball, you'd end up killing it. Our heart is the same way. You cannot pry open someone's heart. But safety is the solution. Remember, God consistently modeled creating safety with us. Compassion is another great reflection of what our heavenly Father does to open our hearts. "The Lord is gracious and righteous; our God is full of compassion" (Psalm 116:5). Jesus also provides us with a wonderful example of how to relate to others with compassion. As Christ ministered, He saw the hearts of His people, and He was moved with compassion to help them. "When he saw the crowds, he had compassion on them, because they were harassed and helpless, like sheep without a shepherd" (Matthew 9:36). We can be like Christ and show compassion to our spouse. "Therefore, as God's chosen people, holy and dearly loved, clothe yourselves with compassion, kindness, humility, gentleness and patience" (Colossians 3:12).

Compassion is caring about our spouse's pain. Compassion is sympathy and kindheartedness. This sets an amazing tone to move deeper into the journey toward intimacy. Compassion communicates that your spouse's heart matters to you. Whatever is going on in his heart—hurt, fear, pain, lies—all of it is important to you. How do you express that you value your spouse's heart? The best way to communicate compassion is to follow Krista's lead—through a kind look, a gentle word, a soft touch, or caring actions. This is why Proverbs 15:1 says, "A gentle answer turns away wrath, but harsh words stir up anger." When you open your heart to your spouse's feelings, you'll get a kinder response in return. King Solomon says: "Patience can persuade a prince, and soft speech can crush strong opposition" (Proverbs 25:15). Care and compassion break down the opposition that was present during the Reactive Cycle and creates two open hearts.

Now that you have created the right atmosphere through emotional safety, you have unlocked the door of healthy conflict. You and your spouse are ready to have an intimate conversation about whatever happened that got you into the Reactive Cycle in the first place. The most effective way to walk through the doorway and into the deepest levels of intimacy is through a powerful communication technique called L.U.V.E. talk.

Nine

L.U.V.E. Talk

Breaking the Reactive Cycle starts with personal responsibility—dealing with you first. This idea is based on the passage of Scripture that says we are hypocrites because we focus on the speck of dust in our spouse's eye instead of removing the log in our own eye. But notice the next part of Matthew 7:5; "then you will see clearly to remove the speck from the other person's eye." We are told to get the log out of our own eye first so we can then respond to our spouse. An important part of personal responsibility is getting your heart open so you can then communicate. After all, a marriage will be only as good as its communication.

However, before you attempt to talk after you've been in the Reactive Cycle, you need to make absolutely sure that your heart is open. This is why King Solomon wrote, "The heart of the righteous weighs its answers" (Proverbs 15:28) and "a wise man's heart guides his mouth" (Proverbs 16:23). There is even an old African proverb that says, "Just keep your heart open to them as you speak your truth." All of this advice points to one truth: Healthy, productive communication requires two open hearts.

Listening is an attitude of the heart, a genuine desire to be with another which both attracts and heals.

—J. ISHAM

I trust that by now you understand this reality. I love Jesus' communication advice; it's exactly what I'm talking about: "Out of the abundance of the heart his mouth speaks" (Luke 6:45). Just like Christ is suggesting, before we talk to our spouse after unhealthy conflict, our heart needs to be abundantly full of God's love. The only way to get our heart full of love is to open it and allow God to fill every single nook and cranny. This is what the apostle Paul was talking about when he wrote, "Instead, speaking the truth in love . . ." (Ephesians 4:15). When we speak "in love" what comes out of our mouth is God's character because He is love. When our heart is open and full of God's love, our words are Christ-like—patient, kind, humble, honoring, selfless, calm, forgiving, protecting, trusting, and hopeful. This makes us safe to respond to our spouse.

How can you tell if your heart is open? This is the litmus test for whether you're ready to communicate. As I've carefully studied the heart, I've found some classic signs that someone's heart is open and ready to respond:

- Gentle and tender with words and actions. A closed heart is calloused and rough.
- Emotionally connected. A closed heart is disconnected.
- Interested, focused, and attentive. A closed heart is self-focused.
- Unselfish, considerate, or thoughtful. A closed heart is selfish.
- Sensitive, compassionate, and caring. A closed heart is insensitive and uncaring.
- Good eye contact. A closed heart avoids eye contact.
- Positive body language. A closed heart displays negative body language.
- Open to touch. A closed heart avoids physical contact.
- A spirit of gratitude and appreciation. A closed heart is critical.
- Awareness of your spouse's tremendous value. A closed heart sees only faults.
- Patience. A closed heart is impatient.
- Kindness. A closed heart is mean and cruel.
- Forgiveness. A closed heart holds grudges.
- Humility and a teachable spirit. A closed heart is prideful.
- Curiosity. A closed heart is bored.
- Seeks first to understand. A closed heart wants to be understood first.
- Hopefulness. A closed heart is hopeless.

The real question is, how do *you* know if your heart is open? What is the telltale sign? For me, I know my heart is open when I seek to understand Erin's perspective. The biggest sign of my closed heart is defensiveness. When I'm trying to explain my actions or get Erin to understand how she has misperceived or misinterpreted something I did, I know that my heart is shut down. If you can genuinely say that you are open to your spouse, you are ready to respond.

I'm frequently asked if *both* hearts need to be open for you to respond. The answer is yes and no. Although the truth is that you don't need your spouse's heart to be open to respond, if it is still closed, be very, very careful. Ideally, both hearts are open so you can have good communication all around. There are plenty of times when I've gone back to Erin and her heart is still closed. During these times, I need to make it my goal to seek to listen and understand her. If Erin isn't open, I can't have any expectations that she will listen and seek to understand me. Likewise, I would encourage you to proceed with extreme caution if your spouse is closed. And here's why. The verse right after the Matthew passage about getting the log out of your own eye says, "Do not give dogs what is sacred; do not throw your pearls to pigs. If you do, they may trample them under their feet, and then turn and tear you to pieces" (Matthew 7:6).

Since when was an emotional argument won by logic?

—ROBERT A. HEINLEIN

I think Jesus is saying that we shouldn't give something valuable (like our heart and emotions) to someone who isn't able to take great care of it. Just like you wouldn't give your pearls to pigs or dogs (and I'm *not* saying that your husbands and wives are pigs and dogs!), you don't want to share your emotions with your spouse unless his heart is open. Otherwise, she will trample your emotions under her feet and tear your heart to pieces. This is what we are capable of doing (reactions) when our heart is shut down. Hasn't that been your experience?

If you put your heart out to someone who isn't in a place to take great care of it, I guarantee you'll end up emotionally wounded. Your heart and emotions are your responsibility. It's no accident that this verse appears after the personal responsibility passage. Not only is it your job to get your heart open; you've also been given the job of protecting your heart ("above all else, guard your heart"). This is why you don't share your heart with someone who is closed. Too often I've watched people throw their feelings before closed hearts only to walk away with a broken heart. That doesn't protect you or your marriage. You can always listen to your spouse's heart, but you must make sure he is open if you're going to share your heart.

The good news is that the more you listen, the greater the odds are that your spouse will start to open to you as well. This is why King Solomon wrote, "A gentle answer turns away wrath" (Proverbs 15:1). Here is how you make this truth practical. Erin and I have made it a rule that we will never discuss sensitive issues unless both of our hearts are open. Before we are willing to talk about the Reactive Cycle, we will say something like this: "I'm feeling pretty open, and I'm ready to talk. Are you open?" If we both acknowledge open hearts, then we will both share. If Erin says that she's still shut down, then I have to make a choice: I can say something like "I'm ready to talk, so let me know when you are ready"—putting the ball in her court, letting her be responsible for her—and then patiently wait until she is ready. My job then is to keep my heart open and ready to talk when she comes back. My other option is to jump into the listener role. I'm not going to put my heart and feelings out there, but I can certainly listen and seek to understand Erin. This may even help her to get open.

The best way to respond and communicate with your spouse is to "L.U.V.E. talk." What's amazing about this powerful communication method is that each of the five steps is designed to take you from unhealthy conflict into deeper levels of intimacy. Remember that healthy conflict is the doorway to intimacy, and here is where you get to watch that truth unfold. If handled in healthy ways, conflict is an opportunity for growth in understanding and for a strengthening of the relationship. Let's jump on it!

Lower your voice and strengthen your argument.

—LEBANESE PROVERB

L.U.V.E. TALK

Once your heart is open and a safe environment has been established, the next step in your journey from the Reactive Cycle to healthy conflict is to communicate using the L.U.V.E. talk method. This is a powerful five-step communication process that stands for *L*isten, *U*nderstand, *V*alidate, *E*mpathize, and *A*pologize (the "a" in "talk"). The door is open; are you ready to walk through into the deepest levels of intimacy and connection? Let's take the first step.

L—Listen

We often hear our spouse, but do we really listen? Researchers say that "It's estimated that people screen out or misunderstand the intended message in over 70 percent of communications, making listening the biggest contributing factor to miscommunication."[1] This means that 70 percent of communication is *mis*communication. Let that sink in. The communication experts are saying that when you talk, there is a 70 percent chance that you are miscommunicating. So, what is the secret to good communication? A young girl with a big heart illustrates the answer best.

Arthur had recently lost his wife of fifty years. To no one's surprise, he was so heartbroken that he couldn't do anything. He had lost the will to live. One day a neighbor's young daughter saw how sad Arthur looked, just sitting on the porch staring out into space. She quickly ran over to visit him.

Arthur was delighted and told the girl's family that she had touched his heart and revived his will to live.

"What did she say?" her parents asked, intrigued.

"Nothing," Arthur explained. "She just sat with me."

To truly listen is one of the greatest gifts that we can give someone. Theologian and philosopher Paul Tillich wrote, "The first responsibility of love is to listen." I think this is why James encouraged us to focus on listening: "My dear brothers, take note of this: Everyone should be quick to listen, slow to speak" (James 1:19). The first step toward the deepest levels of intimacy within your communication is to do what this young girl modeled—be present.

Webster's Dictionary defines listening as hearing with intention; hearing attentively.[2] In other words, the key to listening is to be fully present. My favorite word picture of this idea is the Chinese character that represents "to listen," which is made up of four separate characters joined together: "eyes," "ear," "undivided attention," and "open heart." This perfectly captures the essence of being present. It reminds us of what Saint Benedict wrote; "Listen and attend with the ear of your heart." Beyond just using our ears, it expands the definition of listening to mean something that we do with our whole body. It's so important, when we listen to our spouse, that we use our eyes, ears, attention, and open heart. That is the difference between simply hearing and truly listening. One of my favorite quotes about listening is from Norm Wright: "One of the greatest gifts we can give to our spouse is the gift of listening. It can be an act of love and caring. But far too many couples only hear one another. Few actually listen."[3]

True listening requires you to be fully present—clearly and intentionally focused on your spouse. Author David Benner, in his book *Sacred Companions,* talks about how to give attention and be present.

> To be present to you means that I must be prepared, temporarily, to be absent to me. I must therefore set aside all the things I carry with me in consciousness all day long—my planning for what comes next, my evaluation of how I am doing and my reflection on what is presently transpiring. These are the noises that drown out what is presently transpiring. These are the noises that drown out silence. These are the distractions that keep me focused on myself and make it impossible for me to be present to another person. Presence is enormously difficult. I confess that I sometimes find it easier simply to pretend to be present—to maintain appropriate eye contact, to do more listening than talking and to minimize any appearance of wandering thoughts. It's so tempting to believe that faking presence is an acceptable alternative to offering genuine presence. But it isn't.[4]

Intent focus shows that your whole heart, soul, mind, and body are present, saying that there is nothing else more important in this moment. Jesus encouraged us to "Give your entire attention to what God is doing right now, and don't get worked up about what may or may not happen tomorrow" (Matthew 6:34; The Message). Jesus' point is for us to give 100 percent attention to God in the moment. We must give complete attention to our spouse as well if we want her to feel safe and open her heart to us. Your spouse will know you are listening when you:

- Turn toward him and give eye contact
- Offer your undivided attention, put what you have been doing out of sight and out of mind
- Resist distractions or any other activity that might take you out of the moment (i.e., cell phone or TV)
- Concentrate on what she is saying, but pay extra attention to her heart—feelings and emotion
- Watch nonverbal cues and body language
- Use encouraging and reassuring gestures and body language, such as "I see" or "That's interesting," occasionally smiling and nodding
- Resist thinking about your reply or rebuttal
- Don't get sidetracked by whether you agree with what he is saying
- Let her finish talking before you respond

These behaviors demonstrate a wholehearted presence. However, the single greatest barrier to listening is when your buttons get pushed. As you seek to listen, your expectation should be that your buttons will get pushed. It's not a matter of *if*; it's a matter of *when*. This is a reality because, in addition to sharing feelings, your spouse is going to share facts and opinions. Although someone's feelings are not debatable, facts and opinions are. Don't get sucked into a debate about who's right or wrong, what really happened, or who's to blame or at fault. Don't go there! Try to center the conversation on your spouse's feelings. But remember, you can't keep your spouse from pushing your buttons. It will happen. Therefore, make your attitude "No problem," then take the time to get your heart back open.

Are you ready to go deeper? Listening helps you hear your spouse's wounded heart. Now you're ready to take the next step in L.U.V.E. talk by understanding what happened that pushed your spouse's buttons. Seeking to understand before being understood will move you into an even deeper level of intimacy. Keep going!

Love is saying "I feel differently" instead of "You're wrong."

—BRANDI SNYDER

U—UNDERSTAND

Communication is difficult! One morning Tom found that the battery in his brand-new car had died because he'd left the lights on overnight. He quickly ran back inside the house to ask his wife, Tracy, to help him start the car. Since Tom was in a hurry to get to work on time, he decided against taking the extra time to use the jumper cables.

"You get into your car"—he pointed to Tracy's prehistoric oversize gas-guzzler—"and push my car."

"Do you think that's a good idea?" Tracy asked, somewhat perplexed.

"It's the fastest way," Tom quickly explained while getting back into his car. "Since I have an automatic transmission, you'll need to push me going at least thirty miles an hour for it to start. Now hurry . . . I'm going to be late!"

"Wait . . . How?" Tracy tried to ask as Tom's door shut. "Men!" she yelled while rolling her eyes in the exasperated way that most women do in response to their husband's crazy ideas.

Tom impatiently tapped on his steering wheel as Tracy slowly started her car and drove off.

Tom started fuming as he watched Tracy disappear around the corner. "Where is she going?" he wondered. "Doesn't she realize that I'm in a hurry?"

After about thirty seconds, Tracy's car finally appeared in the rearview mirror.

However, Tom's eyes widened in horror as he helplessly watched Tracy drive straight at him. It was at that exact moment that he realized he probably should have been clearer with his instructions.

The only sound that could be heard as Tracy slammed into his new car going thirty miles an hour—precisely as he'd instructed— was "Nooooooo!"

The way to the heart is through the ears.

—KATIE HURLEY

Amazingly, this is a true story, and one that perfectly illustrates how challenging communication can be as we seek to understand our spouse. That shouldn't be news to anyone in a significant relationship.

The communication experts say that up to 80 percent of our conflicts occur as the result of misunderstandings.[5] This is why, when responding to our spouse, we need to choose to make our primary goal understanding rather than being understood. King Solomon seemed to love the concept of understanding as well: "Though it costs you all you have, get understanding" (Proverbs 4:7). Earlier in the same book, he tells us to "apply our hearts to understanding" (Proverbs 2:2). The point of his advice is that we need to apply our hearts to understanding—especially to our spouse's feelings. Even one of Christ's disciples, Peter, added his two cents when he encouraged husbands around this idea of understanding: "In the same way, you husbands should live with your wives in an understanding way, since they are weaker than you. But show them respect, because God gives them the same blessing he gives you—the grace that gives true life. Do this so that nothing will stop your prayers" (1 Peter 3:7, NCV). You don't need a seminary degree to understand the point of this verse. The lack of honor and understanding can lead to broken communication with God. That's a serious problem! Finally, David Olson did a massive research study with more than fifty thousand couples and discovered that communicating to understand was the number one strength in determining marital success.[6] Trust me, understanding our spouse is extremely important in breaking the Reactive Cycle.

So, how do we practically apply understanding with our spouse? It's actually quite simple. The key to understanding our spouse is through curiosity. The great American poet Walt Whitman summed it up best when he wrote, "Be curious, not judgmental." Instead of judging or ignoring our spouse's emotions, we always have the opportunity to be curious about her feelings—her heart. Curiosity leads to discovery. You learn new things about your spouse when you choose to be curious. King Solomon understood this when he wrote, "The purposes of a man's heart are deep waters, but a man of understanding draws them out" (Proverbs 20:5). How can these deep waters be drawn out? By consistently using the phrase "help me understand." I know it doesn't sound glitzy, but it is effective. This powerful statement is a shift from reacting to trying to connect and care. It will help your spouse's heart to feel safe, and he will begin to open up.

We have two ears and one mouth so that we can listen twice as much as we speak.

—EPICTETUS

Now the conversation is situated perfectly to go to the next level and take your intimacy even deeper. You're ready to validate each other. What a powerful experience you're in for.

V—VALIDATE

Validation is an opportunity to communicate that your spouse's heart and emotions are important to you, regardless of whether you agree or they make sense to you. When you validate your spouse, you recognize, value, and accept his heart—his deepest thoughts, opinions, ideas, beliefs, and emotions.

Invalidation, on the other hand, is to reject, debate, minimize, demean, judge, or try to fix someone's emotions. Invalidation is what happens in the movie *Gaslight,* a 1944 mystery-thriller starring Charles Boyer and Ingrid Bergman as husband and wife Gregory and Paula. Once married, the couple returns to a home inherited by Paula from her aunt, who was mysteriously murdered in the house. Once they have moved in, Gregory, who is in reality a jewel thief and the murderer of Paula's aunt, tries to convince his wife that she is going mad. His plan is to have her certified insane and institutionalized, so he can find the priceless jewels hidden in the attic. Though Paula is certain that she sees the house's gaslights dim every evening and that there are strange noises coming from the attic, Gregory convinces Paula that she's imagining things. The film has a classic Hollywood ending when Paula is rescued in dramatic fashion. What I find fascinating about the film is that it birthed a psychological term called "gaslighting." Counselors use the expression to describe efforts to gradually manipulate someone into doubting her own reality or to trick a person into believing she is insane. Gaslighting is a great demonstration of invalidation. We gaslight or invalidate our spouse in many ways—some intentional, some unintentional:

- You're so sensitive.
- Your feelings are wrong.
- That's ridiculous. You shouldn't feel that way.
- It's no big deal. Why do you get so emotional?
- It's just your time of the month!
- Lighten up. You're overreacting.
- You're so dramatic. Your emotions are out of control.
- You're crazy! That's not how you really feel.
- Can't you take a joke?
- Relax. Stop freaking out!
- You are not being very rational.
- It's nothing to get upset over. You shouldn't let it bother you.
- You should be over that by now.[7]

That is a pretty sobering list. When I first read through these invalidating statements, I cringed as I realized how many of the phrases I use with my loved ones—especially Erin. Sadly, I'm sure

I've sent the message to Erin that not only were her *feelings* wrong, but there was something wrong with *her*. This is the gaslighting part of what I was unintentionally doing to my wife, as Steve Hein explained:

No one wants to feel that something is fundamentally wrong with them. Sadly, in the end, invalidation goes beyond mere rejection by implying not only that our feelings are wrong, but that we are abnormal. This implies that there is something fundamentally wrong with us because we aren't like our spouse; we are strange; we are different; we are weird.[8]

Invalidation quickly closes a heart. The good news is that there is an antidote. Validation is when we safely allow our spouse to share her thoughts and feelings. The message is that it's okay to think or feel the way she does. Validation is when we help our spouse feel unconditionally accepted.

Listen and attend with the ear of your heart.

—SAINT BENEDICT

Most of us truly want to validate our spouse when he is frustrated or hurting, but often we don't know how, or we start giving advice. I have found that, usually, if I validate Erin, she is able to work out her own emotional problems faster than if I give her advice. To be honest, this can be difficult for me, because Erin's emotions or perspectives often push my buttons. I get defensive or go into fix-it mode so quickly that it keeps me from validating her. To battle my natural tendency to debate and problem solve Erin's feelings, I have to remind myself of that Teddy Roosevelt quote, "People don't care what you know until they know that you care." I have to constantly remember that Erin won't care about my perspective, my emotions, or my idea of a solution until she feels that I care about her. This is the opposite of gaslighting. Thus, I've found that there are three powerful ways to validate our spouse.

1. REPEAT BACK WHAT YOU HEAR YOUR SPOUSE SAYING

A great deal of validation occurs if you get good at reflecting or repeating back what your spouse is saying:

- So what I hear you saying is _____.
- Is that what you are saying _____?
- Am I understanding you right?
- It sounds like _____ is really important to you.
- So what bothered you was that _____?

What stops us from making these validating statements? Some people have a difficult time reflecting back what their spouse is saying because they fear it means they agree with that perspective or interpretation of the facts. Don't forget, validation says, "You matter to me, regardless of whether or not I agree with your perspective or whether or not your feelings make sense to me." When you disagree with the facts or opinions that your spouse is sharing, the key is to focus on her feelings and emotions. Watch how it works.

2. ACKNOWLEDGE THE UNDERLYING EMOTION

Another reason communication is so challenging is that the words we use are only a small part of the message our spouse hears. For example, one study found that your tone of voice comprises 38 percent of communication, and 55 percent is body language. Thus, only 7 percent of communication is determined by the words we speak.[9] And yet most of us stay religiously focused on the words our spouse is speaking, and we miss the other 93 percent. Do you think this is why King Solomon warned, "Do not pay attention to every word people say"? (Ecclesiastes 7:21). The words we use can pose a major challenge in our communication process, as Michael McMillan explained:

> The dictionary doesn't define words—people do. We each create the meaning they carry. Words mean different things to different people at different times and places. And yet many of us are very committed to analyzing and scrutinizing the words, opinions and facts that our spouse shares.[10]

I can debate for hours the particulars, specifics, figures, statements, and events as Erin sees them. This gets us nowhere fast, and we both walk away feeling disconnected. However, I always have the option of focusing on Erin's emotions. Her feelings are not debatable. They are what they are—the voice of her heart. I can choose to care about her heart. This not only helps her to feel safe; it takes us to a much deeper level of intimacy. To understand your spouse's emotions, try using phrases like these:

- That sounds frustrating . . . that sounds discouraging . . . that sounds like it would really hurt . . . that must have been scary.
- How strongly are you feeling that (on a scale of 0 to 10)?

- So you really felt _____?
- It sounds like you are really feeling _____.
- How else did you feel?
- How did you feel when _____ happened?

This kind of questioning helps validate our spouse's feelings. But when we question, disagree, debate, or argue with how he feels, we completely invalidate our spouse. These behaviors only push us further apart and keep the Reactive Cycle spinning around. On the other hand, it's extremely powerful when we allow our spouse to experience her feelings and validate her emotions. The final component of validation is acceptance.

3. ACCEPT THEIR FEELINGS AND PERSPECTIVE

Once you understand your spouse's perspective and emotions, you can then follow the reflective listening with a simple statement like:

- It makes sense to me that you are feeling that way.
- I know just what you mean.
- I would feel the same way.
- I can understand why you feel that way.
- What you are saying matters to me.
- Your feelings are really important.

When one spouse does not object to or argue with the other's feelings, but instead accepts her with validation, the other spouse feels truly loved. One spouse's validating attitude confirms that his spouse has a right to feel the way he does. Remember, we can validate our spouse's point of view while possessing a different viewpoint. When I say, "Erin, I really understand that you are hurting, that this has wounded you," I am not necessarily saying, "Erin, I agree with you, and I was wrong." Rather, I am saying, "I could tell that this really hurt you, and your feelings mean the world to me. I care how you feel!" It's also important that we verbally communicate that we are with our spouse, on the same page, and on the same team. In the end, you will find that validation opens hearts.

Empathy is seeing with the eyes of another, listening with the ears of another, and feeling with the heart of another.

—ALFRED ADLE

Healthy conflict is a doorway to intimacy. And the first step toward that intimacy is listening with our whole body. Being present drives us deeper relationally as we seek to understand our spouse before being understood. The more we listen and validate our spouse's thoughts and feelings, the more connected we feel. The final step toward true intimacy and deep connection is one of the greatest gifts we can give. The deepest level of intimacy we can reach in a relationship is when we empathize with our spouse.

E—EMPATHY

Empathy is entering into another person's world and feeling with that person, rather than feeling sorry for her. This is what the apostle Paul was encouraging us to do when he wrote, "Carry each other's burdens" (Galatians 6:2). Empathy is more than feeling sorry that your spouse is burdened or troubled. Empathy takes place as you carry your spouse's burdens. It says, "I feel your pain." Do you see the difference between the third step and the fourth step of caring? Validation says, "Your feelings matter to me"; empathy says, "I feel what you feel." Validation is great, but it doesn't allow us to go to the deepest level of intimacy. Empathy, on the other hand, expresses connection on a much deeper emotional level. Both empathy and validation are essential, but empathy is the greatest gift we can give our spouse. Watch how Christ modeled giving the gift of empathy with His close friends when his good friend Lazarus died. "When Jesus saw her [Mary] weeping, and the Jews who had come along with her also weeping, he was deeply moved in spirit and troubled. 'Where have you laid him?' he asked. 'Come and see, Lord,' they replied. Jesus wept" (John 11: 33–35).

Isn't it fascinating how the shortest verse in the Bible, "Jesus wept," is also the best illustration of empathy? I'm convinced that Jesus knew He was going to raise Lazarus from the dead. I don't think this miracle was a knee-jerk, impulsive decision: "Hey, wait a minute. I totally forgot I could raise Lazarus from the dead! What was I thinking?" Instead, Jesus already had the perfect solution in mind for the problem He encountered. This is why I've always been so fascinated with why Jesus didn't try to calm the family down when he found them weeping and agonizing over the loss of their brother. If it had been me, I'd have said something like, "Relax. It's me, Jesus. You know, the Son of God. Stop crying and watch what I'm about to do. In about sixty seconds, you are about to see the coolest miracle your eyes have ever seen!"

*When you talk, you repeat what you already know;
when you listen, you often learn something.*

—JARED SPARKS

Instead of trying to relieve their pain by talking about the solution or how He was going to fix the problem, Jesus modeled empathy. Jesus wept. Isn't it interesting that after Christ's empathy, the Jewish people watching exclaimed, "See how he loved him!" (John 11:36). Thousands of years before Teddy Roosevelt, Jesus knew that people don't care what you know until they know that you care. Empathy is the deepest level of caring.

How do you put empathy into action? It's actually quite simple.

First, allow your open heart to be touched by the pain of others; Jesus was "deeply moved in spirit." Next, allow your heart to experience what your spouse is feeling; Jesus wept with them. Finally, don't try to end their pain; follow Christ's example and just sit with your spouse's emotions. We don't need to fix their feelings or move them beyond their pain. Romans 12:15 provides great advice: "Rejoice with those who rejoice; mourn with those who mourn." Certainly, Jesus raised Lazarus from the dead, but He took the time to mourn and empathize with his friends first. When Erin is hurting, she does not want me to ignore her and pretend nothing is going on. She doesn't want me to say, "Snap out of it!" She doesn't want me to compare her situation to that of the less fortunate. Erin wants me to mourn with her, experience her emotions, feel her pain, put myself in her shoes, and see things from her perspective. The bottom line is, Erin wants me to care about her heart. Listening helps me to understand and validate her emotions. Empathy, however, allows me access to the deepest levels of intimacy by saying, "I feel with you." This reminds me of one of my favorite quotes by Maya Angelou, "People will forget what you said, people will forget what you did, but people will never forget how you made them feel."

Listen or your tongue will keep you deaf.

—NATIVE AMERICAN PROVERB

The greatest gift we can give our spouse is empathy, because it's the deepest level of intimacy we can reach with a person. When we analyze, scrutinize, debate, and question our spouse's feelings, we simple trade places in the head. Empathizing—deeply feeling what your spouse feels—trades places in the heart. Walt Whitman wrote, "I do not ask the wounded person how he feels, I become the wounded person." That's a wonderful picture of empathy.

Scottish people talk about falling in love as "having a soft heart." This is exactly what empathy does to a heart—it softens it. Once your heart has become soft and pliable, you are ready for the final act of L.U.V.E. talk. So that we stay consistent with our phrase L.U.V.E. talk, let's say that the "a" in talk stands for apology.

a—APOLOGIZE

Jim and Suzette were involved in a petty argument, both unwilling to admit they might be in error.

"I'll admit I'm wrong," Suzette told her husband in a conciliatory attempt, "if you'll admit I'm right."

Jim agreed and, like a gentleman, insisted she go first.

"I'm wrong," Suzette said.

With a twinkle in his eye, Jim responded, "You're right!"

According to new research, people apologize about four times a week. But on average, they offer up these apologies most often to friends (46 percent of the time), then strangers (22 percent), romantic partners (11 percent), and finally, family members (7 percent), with the remaining percentage falling into other categories.[11] Isn't it sad that our spouse and kids are last on the list of those who receive apology? Why is it so hard to admit to our family members that we are wrong and then apologize?

Some people struggle to apologize because of pride and selfishness. For others, never being wrong gives power and moral superiority, or at least the illusion of it. Some individuals can't forgive because they don't want their spouse to forget how much they were hurt. It's like they're thinking, "If I forgive you, you'll forget how much you hurt me, and I'll get wounded again." I think the bottom line is that we have a difficult time apologizing because our heart is still closed.

I was guilty of another issue. My problem was that I got to a place in our marriage where I would instantly offer an apology to Erin the moment we got into an argument. "That's a good thing," you might be thinking. In some ways, you're right. A heartfelt apology based on a deep understanding of how you hurt or frustrated your spouse is a great thing. However, that's not at all what I was doing. I became great at using the words "I'm sorry" to manipulate my wife. Mark Stevens calls this a "fraudulent apology," and it goes something like this: "I don't know why you're unhappy, but I'm sorry." Mark said that during his thirty-five-year marriage, he has sincerely apologized to his wife just five times—but he has said he's sorry an additional 3,500 times. Stevens added, "Ninety percent of apologies are to keep the peace. How can you have a sincere apology if you don't know what you've done?"[12]

I also learned pretty quickly in my marriage that when Erin was upset or frustrated with me, if I simply told her that I was sorry, the conflict would go away. The problem was that I didn't feel convicted or remorseful about what I had done. I was trying to make the uncomfortable situation or the guilty feelings go away. The problem was that my seemingly brilliant strategy never brought us into the levels of deep intimacy that I really wanted. It just put an end to the awkwardness or unpleasantness of conflict. I was trading peace for real intimacy.

A good marriage is the union of two good forgivers.

—RUTH BELL GRAHAM

The good news is that forgiveness accounts for about a third of marriage satisfaction.[13] Think about that for a moment. One third (33 percent) of the happiness in your marriage is from forgiving and being forgiven. That's huge! Another research study found that couples could improve the quality of their marital relationship over time if they applied the principle of forgiveness in their marriage.[14] Not only does forgiveness benefit the quality of a marital relationship, it also has individual benefits. Forgiveness has been shown to improve mental and physical health and life satisfaction.[15]

Do you see how vital forgiveness is in your marriage and to your life? The key is that we need to seek an apology when our heart is open and after we truly understand our spouse's heart. This is why seeking forgiveness is the final step in the journey toward intimacy. It's like the cherry on top of a delicious ice cream sundae.

Let me explain why forgiveness comes at the end. We have no business offering an apology until we've allowed our compassion to drive us toward understanding our spouse's hurt, fear, and frustration. We shouldn't utter the words "I'm sorry" until we've validated and empathized with our spouse. Until we have truly entered into our spouse's hurt and allowed that pain to touch our heart, we have no right to seek forgiveness. We need to be brought to a real understanding of our part of the Reactive Cycle and the consequences of our actions and words. When we reach this place of awareness, our heart is soft and tender. Now we are ready to seek forgiveness. This is exactly what the apostle Paul meant when he encouraged, "Be kind to one another, tenderhearted, forgiving one another, as God in Christ forgave you" (Ephesians 4:32).

The process of a healing apology is made up of four simple statements. Watch how powerful these twelve words can be in helping reach the deepest level of intimacy.

"I was wrong." These first three words acknowledge that you understand your words or actions hurt your spouse, and they validate her pain.

"I am sorry." These next three words go beyond confession and give you the opportunity to explain that not only do you understand how much you hurt your spouse, you also feel terrible about it. The empathy allows you to feel the remorse necessary for the next statement.

"Please forgive me." These words inform your spouse that you accept responsibility for your actions and that you want to see your relationship reconciled. You are not demanding anything; instead, you are inviting him to forgive you and to restore the intimacy and connection that was broken because of the Reactive Cycle. Requesting forgiveness also displays humility from the offender, because you have to admit that you have been wrong and you are willing to make things right.

"I love you!" The final three words affirm your love and commitment to your spouse. They say that your love isn't dependent on whether your spouse forgives you. Instead, you are saying that your love is unconditional and that your heart is fully open.

Mahatma Gandhi stated, "The weak never forgive. Forgiveness is the attribute of the strong." Conflicts, arguments, and offenses are unavoidable, and the inability to forgive becomes a person's personal prison. In order to remain in a loving relationship, you must grasp the idea that forgiveness is essential.

WHEN A SOLUTION OR DECISION IS STILL NEEDED

Most of the time you find that solutions are much less important to the other person than feeling cared for. People don't care how much you *know* until they know how much you *care*. Often understanding, validation, and empathy can end the conflict, even without finding a solution. Most conflicts are resolved when two people feel heard, understood, and validated—when they feel "cared" for. Isn't that encouraging! Most of the time we don't need some elaborate solution. L.U.V.E. talk is going to get us to those deep levels of intimacy and connection that we desire. However, if a solution is needed, the best process is to find something that feels great to *both* of you. Let me show you how to solve your issues as one—as teammates.

Ten

Two Hearts Unified:
Winning Together as a Team

Let's do a quick review of how to fight your way to a better marriage. We began with the realization that every conflict, frustration, or hurtful situation happens because our emotional buttons get pushed. And when our buttons are pushed, our hearts close, and we instantly react. Unfortunately, our reactions only make things worse, because in our reactions, we push our spouse's buttons, their heart shuts down, and then they react. This sequence is called the Reactive Cycle. The good news is that there is a way to break this pattern of unhealthy conflict.

Since it's impossible to have a productive discussion when your heart is closed, the first step in breaking the Reactive Cycle is to "deal with the log in your own eye" and get your own heart back open. You accomplish this by taking a time-out, naming your feelings, and taking your emotions to the Lord to discover the truth.

When your heart is open, you are safe to have a healthy conversation with your spouse. The next step in breaking the Reactive Cycle is to communicate using the L.U.V.E. talk method. This method means that you don't focus on how to fix the issue or solve the problem. Instead, you focus on your spouse's heart, making it your goal to listen, understand, validate, and empathize with how your spouse feels. People don't care what you *know* until they know that you *care*. This type of communication makes a marriage feel safe. And when your spouse feels safe, his heart will most likely be open, enabling you to reach the deepest levels of intimacy and connection. This is the true gift of healthy conflict.

Coming together is a beginning. Keeping together is progress. Working together is success.

—HENRY FORD

The final step in breaking the Reactive Cycle is to problem solve as teammates. This is much easier said than done because of power struggles. A power struggle is when you get into a relational tug-of-war while trying to make a decision. On one hand, disagreement is healthy for a relationship. When Erin and I don't see eye to eye, we have an opportunity to learn something new about each other, or we may uncover issues that need to be dealt with. Remember, healthy conflict is a doorway to deeper intimacy and connection. Sadly, most couples don't effectively manage their differences, and the Reactive Cycle usually explodes into action. When we consistently feel that we are in a never-ending battle while making decisions, the relationship begins to feel adversarial. If we constantly go from being teammates to opponents, marriage will quickly start to feel unsafe. And don't forget, when you feel unsafe, your heart shuts down and you disconnect relationally. This is exactly what Jesus meant when He said, "Any kingdom divided against itself will be ruined, and a house divided against itself will fall" (Luke 11:17). Unhealthy power struggles destroy relationships, because any time you and your spouse square off against each other, the outcome is guaranteed: A marriage divided will fall! Therefore, to avoid power struggles and disunity in your marriage, you need to find a win-win solution.

WIN-WIN SOLUTION

Do you remember when your teacher would spring a pop quiz on you? I still have nightmares about those—pop quizzes could be the reason I graduated near the bottom of my high school class! Well, here is your relationship pop quiz. True or false: In a marriage, a win-win solution is always better than a win-lose solution.

Do you have your answer? Before I give you the correct response, let's talk about the concept of a win-win.

We've all heard the phrase "win-win," right? Even if you don't work in the corporate world or have never been to a Stephen Covey workshop, the idea of a win-win solution has become deeply rooted in our culture. This is something that I've tried to live out in my marriage. When Erin and I are faced with a decision, the best possible solution is a win-win. But let's not just deal with ideals. Let's also talk about reality. I don't know what happens in your marriage, but there are plenty of times in mine when a win-win solution seems virtually impossible. Don't you run into times when you and your spouse want solutions that are on opposite ends of the spectrum?

Of course, a win-win would be nice, but there are times when we end up with a win-lose. Has this ever happened to you? Don't we all wish we lived in the land of "happily ever after," where everything ends up perfect and both people feel like they've won every time? This doesn't feel anything like the world where my marriage exists. Instead, there are plenty of times in my marriage when we have to compromise and make sacrifices for the sake of the relationship. I'm not saying it's bad to put your spouse's desires before your own. Philippians 2:3 says, "Do nothing out of selfish ambition or vain conceit, but in humility consider others better than yourselves." Furthermore, Romans 12:10 says, "Be devoted to one another in brotherly love. Honor one another above yourselves." Many times throughout our marriage, Erin and I have tolerated win-lose decisions. When I "won," I would rationalize, justify, or defend my actions by thinking that Erin simply needed to submit to my authority as the leader of our family. When Erin "won," she would validate and support her choice by thinking that I would warm up to the idea once I realized that her intuition was right once again.

Let me illustrate what I'm talking about by sharing a time when we remodeled our house. Erin was nine months pregnant. Insane, right? Just you wait.

When Erin was pregnant with Garrison, our now-eleven-year-old son, we were living in a home that had three bedrooms. We wanted each child to have his or her own room, so we decided to turn the loft area above our kitchen into a fourth bedroom. Seems simple enough . . .

We started looking for a builder, and everyone we talked to in our tiny community recommended the same guy. "You have to hire Rodney." "Rodney will build a great room." "We used this wonderful builder named Rodney." We quickly accepted the influence of our friends and called Rodney.

Remember, upon the conduct of each depends the fate of all.

—ALEXANDER THE GREAT

I'll never forget the moment when I met Rodney. The doorbell rang, and I opened the door. I'm sure I stood in the foyer with my mouth hanging open and a dumbfounded look on my face. Why, you ask? Well, when I use the phrase "Ozark Mountain Builder," what images get conjured up in your mind? Rodney was one of the biggest men I'd ever laid eyes on. He was wearing overalls, a plaid flannel shirt, and a baseball cap that read "John Deere." He had a long, bushy beard that reminded me of the classic-rock group ZZ Top. Can you see why, when I greeted Rodney, I was a little stunned? He was intimidating to look at, the kind of guy you think has never had a feeling or been aware of an emotion in his entire life. I know what you're thinking: He was the exact opposite of me. Now you're just being cruel.

Anyway, Rodney turned out to be not just a great builder but a nice guy as well. My favorite memory of Rodney happened when our daughter Murphy, who was about three years old at the time, accidentally punk'd him.

I was sitting at the dinner table working one morning while Rodney was busy hammering away in the loft area. Murphy had been in her room playing with some toys when she came toddling toward the balcony near where Rodney was building. "Daddy," she cried out, "do you love me?"

I rolled my eyes in response to her question—not because I didn't love my precious daughter, but because she was going through this phase where she would ask us if we loved her like twelve million times every day. After we would answer yes, she would ask if we were proud of her. She would then cycle through these same two questions until we'd had enough.

"Daddy, do you love me?" Before I could answer Murphy, Rodney started to laugh. I'm not sure what was so funny; maybe it was her display of emotion that had tickled Rodney.

"Yes, sweetie," I responded, shaking my head at Rodney, "I love you."

"Daddy," Murphy then asked, "are you proud of me?" Again, before I could respond, Rodney laughed even harder. This was one calloused man!

"Yes, honey," I answered. "Daddy is very proud of you!"

"Daddy," Murphy started again. I knew the cycle was going to spin around about twenty more times and that I would have to endure Rodney's taunting laughter for several more minutes. But I was in for a pleasant surprise.

"Daddy," Murphy asked, "do you love Rodney?" Before I could answer her question, Rodney coughed and dropped his hammer. It was as if someone had used one of those defibrillators on his cold heart. I quickly jumped at the opportunity. "Yes," I said, "I love Rodney a lot!"

United we stand; divided we fall.

—AESOP

I then had the privilege of listening to this full-grown "mountain man" attempt to explain to a three-year-old how it was okay for two guys to love each other. "Am I hearing you right, Rodney," I yelled out, "you love me, too?" I think that was the point when Rodney fell off his ladder in full cardiac arrest.

After Rodney's heart grew three sizes bigger, like the Grinch, or maybe it was that he got in touch with his sensitive side, he finished the room.

The day arrived when Erin and I were going to move stuff into the new bedroom. Have you ever had that experience when you and your spouse talk through how to solve a problem, but when it comes time to execute the plan, something very different happens? That's exactly what happened to us. While I thought we had decided which child was going into the new bedroom, when it came time to move the furniture, I was confused by what Erin was doing. Like we had concluded, I started to move in Taylor's (our oldest child) stuff, but I ran into Erin in the hallway, dragging Garrison's (the baby) stuff toward the room.

"What are you doing?" I asked.

"What do you mean?" Erin said. "I'm taking Garrison's belongings into his new room."

"The one we just built?" I responded while pointing at the new room.

"Yes," Erin countered, "just like we decided."

"That wasn't the decision. We agreed that this was Taylor's room. Remember? This is such a great room that we determined Taylor would really enjoy it. As a baby, Garrison doesn't care where he is. We could put him in a closet, and he'd be happy!" (For the record, I've never actually done that, so don't call the authorities!) Erin and I cycled around for a few more minutes before we both gave up in defeat.

So, Mr. Stephen Covey, how do you reach a win-win solution in this situation? You see, this is the real world that I was talking about. Although Erin and I wanted a win-win, we also know that in reality it's not always that simple. She wanted Garrison in that new bedroom, and I wanted Taylor. How do you solve this one? Either way, someone is going to lose.

Does this ever happen to you? Let's go back to the pop quiz you took. Remember, the question was: True or false, in a marriage, a win-win solution is always better than a win-lose solution. The correct answer is actually false. Did you get it right? Don't worry if you guessed wrong. Even though you now have a zero, which means you are currently failing the marriage quiz, I'll give you some extra-credit work that can be done only with your spouse in the privacy of your own bedroom!

The truth is that most people fail this quiz. Even though the statement "a win-win is always better than a win-lose" sounds true, there is something wrong with it. What makes this statement false is something minuscule that often goes unnoticed, and yet it has weakened or destroyed many marriages. The truth is that in marriage, there is no such thing as a win-lose. Since you are married and on the same team, you either win together or you lose together. There is no other option. This understanding literally changed my marriage. Although Erin and I believed we were on the same team, we often didn't act like it. So many times, when attempting to make a decision (like with the new bedroom), we abandoned our marriage team and ended up as adversaries. And make no mistake, any time one team member loses, the entire team loses.

A true win-win mind-set says members of the same team win together or they lose together; therefore, in a marriage, I can't win unless my spouse also wins. As Erin and I put this amazing truth into practice, we changed how we made decisions. We started to make it unacceptable for either person to walk away from any decision-making interaction feeling as if he or she had lost. Erin and I agreed to define win-win as finding a solution that we both feel great about. This is the same thing the apostle Paul encouraged us to do:

"Each of you should look not only to your own interests, but also to the interests of others" (Philippians 2:4). Do you see the win-win? In plain and simple language, Paul is describing a win-win. We are being told to look not only to our own interests (win) but also to the interests of the other person (win). If you are going to make this idea work in your marriage, you must redefine winning as finding a solution that both of you feel good about.

Convincing yourself doesn't win an argument.

—ROBERT HALF

"Yeah, right!" you might be thinking. "Finding a solution that feels good to both people. No way! It looks great on paper, but it will never work in the real world." Well, what other option do you have? Let's revisit Matthew 12:25, where Jesus insists, "Every kingdom divided against itself will be ruined, and every city or household divided against itself will not stand." That's pretty clear! A house divided will fall. It doesn't say "might" or "may." It's a definitive "will." In the end, nothing takes more time or creates more problems in your marriage than failure. Robert Alan Silverstein explains it this way:

> Conflicts are a normal part of life; how we deal with them can make a big difference. Often when people resolve conflicts, one person ends up a winner, and one loses out. This may solve the problem for the moment, but resentment and bad feelings can cause more problems later. Another way to look at

conflicts is to try to find a WIN-WIN solution, in which both sides can benefit. In this way, conflicts are turned into opportunities to grow and make things better.[1]

Your house—your marriage—will fall if your focus is on defending your point of view and sticking to your idea of the solution. And this relational tug-of-war will continue until someone grows weary and gives up. I've counseled couples who have been arguing about the same thing for over twenty years. Seriously. I'm not a math whiz, but that sounds like a colossal waste of time. The reality is that while the win-win process may take more time and effort in the beginning, it can save you decades of frustration and relational pain.

The more arguments you win, the fewer friends you will have.

—AMERICAN PROVERB

Erin and I had a choice to make that day when deciding which child to put in the new bedroom. We could have agreed that the only acceptable solution was one that we both felt great about. Unfortunately, we had chosen an adversarial path that resulted in our team losing. I think we reached a point of exhaustion from losing over and over. Our team was worn out emotionally. We knew we needed to do something different, and that difference came in the form of the win-win decision-making process.

FIVE STEPS TO A WIN-WIN SOLUTION

But how do you implement this amazing strategy in your marriage? I promise that it's much easier than you think. The key is to follow five simple steps. By the way, the process works regardless of the conflict. I'll prove it by returning to the bedroom story and show you how we eventually discovered a solution that we both felt great about. You might be surprised by who ended up in the room.

Once Erin and I reached an impasse, we both turned around and returned the stuff we were holding to its original location. Over the next few days, we tried to make a decision, but unfortunately, nothing worked. We weren't in a major fight, but we were annoyed with each other and frustrated that we couldn't agree on a solution.

Wouldn't you know it, to once again illustrate that God has a sense of humor, we were scheduled to teach a marriage seminar that weekend. Take one guess what they wanted us to talk about. How to make decisions as a couple. I'm dead serious!

As we drove to the seminar city, we talked about what we were going to teach. When we talk about decision making, we often involve the audience in a fun exercise. We list several recent conflicts on different pieces of paper, then place them in an old John Deere cap (in honor of Rodney!) or bowl so that someone from the audience can pick one. After the person selects a particular fight, we act it out and demonstrate how to work through the issue toward a solution. It's actually quite fun; people seem to enjoy watching me look like an idiot!

*The aim of argument, or of discussion, should not be
victory, but progress.*

—JOSEPH JOUBERT

While we were driving, Erin and I started to brainstorm different arguments that we could use, and she wrote them on small pieces of paper. We had come up with about five different examples when she suggested that we include the new-bedroom conflict.

"No way!" I shot back.

"Why not?" Erin asked, surprised by my sudden reaction.

"Because we haven't resolved the issue," I explained. "We'll sound like a couple of phonies. Don't write that one down."

By the way, this is one more example of how Erin and I remember things differently. She would tell you that she didn't say what I'm about to tell you. But trust me when I tell you that I clearly remember Erin saying she wouldn't include that conflict in our selection process.

Fast-forward to our session. There we were, up onstage in front of about three hundred people. We came to the part when Erin placed our folded conflict papers into a bowl and asked an audience member to pick one. Well, use your imagination and take one guess at what the person read out loud. That's right, the new-bedroom conflict! I'm sure I looked like a complete moron when I said to this poor guy, "I'm sorry, but what did you just say?" in a stern voice.

He sheepishly looked down, carefully reread the paper, and slowly answered, "The new-bedroom conflict." Like reading it slow was going to change anything.

I was shocked. To make matters worse (as if they could get any worse), Erin stepped forward and said, "You may be wondering why all of the color has drained from Greg's face." I shook my head in disbelief. "Greg didn't want me to use this conflict," Erin continued, "because we haven't resolved the issue. But I think that we have no business coaching you guys if we can't make this technique work for our own marriage." I'll concede that she had a good point, but I still insist that she promised me she wouldn't put it in the bowl. Actually, if you want another illustration of my wife's fun and playful sense of humor, take one guess at what was written on every slip of paper. That's right—the phrase "new-bedroom conflict."

Let me show you how we got from this point to a win-win solution. Instead of dancing around the decision, compromising, or losing together, we moved through the steps to find a solution that we both felt thrilled about. The great news is that you can do the same thing in your own marriage. Here we go.

If you want to make peace with your enemy, you have to work with your enemy. Then he becomes your partner.

—NELSON MANDELA

1. Verbalize Your Mutual Desire for a Win-Win Solution

The best place to begin is by reminding each other that you are on the same team. Reiterate that the only acceptable solution is something that feels great to both people. By reaffirming this desire, you instantly create a safe environment. When people aren't worried about protecting their own agenda, defending their position, getting walked on, or being taken advantage of, they relax. When you are no longer anxious that your feelings and ideas won't be considered, the worry disappears and is replaced by hope. When you believe that your spouse also wants what is best for you, your heart opens, and this paves the way for creativity. That is the key to finding a win-win solution—you need to have the creative juices flowing. But that will happen only when two hearts are open. And hearts open only when they feel safe.

When Erin and I started to talk about the new bedroom, I said to her, "Remember, the only acceptable solution is something that we both feel great about." I explained to my wife that I wasn't going to convince her or manipulate her into any decision. Try this the next time you find yourself in a power struggle with your spouse. You'll be amazed at how verbalizing that you're on the same team can create a positive climate to finding a win-win solution. As a matter of fact, if this is all you do the next time you're trying to make a joint decision, I guarantee that you will see an enormous improvement in your relationship.

The law of win-win says, "Let's not do it your way or my way; let's do it the best way."

—GREG ANDERSON

Once hearts are open and relaxed, you are ready for the next step.

2. Discover the "Win" for Each Person

This is where you will spend 80 percent of your time. Remember from the last chapter that your job was to care for each other's hearts. Caring is an amazing gift that we give to our spouses. But this step is not about empathy. The focus is not on feelings and emotions; instead, it's on trying to understand the win for each person. You are trying to pinpoint what your spouse really wants. You are here because you both have a particular solution that you think is the best way to resolve the conflict. Your mission is to understand what both people want. Don't forget James 4:1: "What causes fights and quarrels among you? Don't they come from your desires that battle within you?" It's your unmet desires and wants that are causing the conflict in the first place. Thus, you need to bring them to the surface. To find out what people want, view their desires as buried treasure—you'll need to dig for them.

Here lies the problem. As I've worked with thousands of couples over the years, I've noticed something that keeps most of them from discovering a win-win solution. What we offer as an initial solution to the conflict often has nothing to do with what we want down deep. Why? Most people don't seem to know what they really want. Many people are so out of touch with themselves, their hearts, and their emotions that they've lost the ability to perceive their real needs and wants. Others have become so numb that they are unaware of their natural yearnings and desires. In the end, nothing gets resolved, and couples remain stuck. If we are going to resolve our conflicts, we must understand our deepest desires. What are the wishes, wants, hopes, and dreams that battle deep down within you? That is what you must discover.

How do you uncover deeper wants and desires? One word: curiosity. During this step, it's extremely important to maintain an attitude of curiosity. If you're going after heart desires, you must keep hearts open. When you approach your spouse with true curiosity, this step feels safe. If both people have this attitude, you are able to clarify what you both want. More important, you'll need the information for the next steps. Asking questions is the way in which you put curiosity into action: What is it that you really want? What will your solution help you to accomplish? Why is your solution so important?

Think of the curiosity process as a funnel. You want to sift through a lot of material to pare down to what each person really wants. To discover this, take turns repeating back your spouse's proposed solution, then ask why it is so important to him. Don't attempt to convince your spouse why her ideas are wrong, stupid, illogical, or won't work. Just listen. Never argue or debate his solution. Don't try to manipulate your spouse toward your solution, or you'll end up with a loss for your team!

Watch how this works.

Choose one person to go first. In our new-bedroom conflict, Erin and I decided that she would start our win-win process. After all, I didn't want to talk about it in front of three hundred of our new best friends. The best way to figure out what Erin really wanted was to start with her original proposed solution. Remember, she wanted Garrison (the baby) in the new room.

"Help me understand why having Garrison in the bedroom is so important?" I asked. It's important to ask questions in a curious tone. If my questions sound like I'm debating or judging her ideas, Erin will go into defensive mode or will shut down. Remember, you are trying to keep your spouse's heart open while you figure out her half of the win-win, so be careful. Here are some other questions that I could ask along the way:

If Garrison went into the new room . . .

. . . why is that such a win for you?

. . . what would it help accomplish in your eyes?

. . . how would it make you feel?

. . . . why does this really matter to you?

"I just think Garrison is the best choice," Erin replied. Since I don't want to argue her logic, debate her thinking, or ask her to consider other ideas, I need to explore each statement that she makes and drill deeper.

"What is it about Garrison being in that room that makes him the best choice?" I asked.

"Well," Erin said thoughtfully, "he has so much stuff, and the new room is so big."

I was tempted to debate that our oldest daughter had more stuff than Garrison, but I didn't want to shut Erin down. "How does that help you if he has more space for his stuff?"

"It helps me to keep his room better organized," Erin continued, "and that would allow me to manage him much faster."

"So, more space helps you go faster?" I asked. "Is that what you really want, a quicker way to manage Garrison?"

"Yes."

Now we were getting somewhere.

"So is that your real win," I asked, "a faster way to manage Garrison?"

"That's important," Erin explained, "but that's not what I really want."

We continued to talk for a few more minutes until Erin said, "I just think that Garrison has the most need for that space."

"So you want whoever has the most needs to be in the room?" I asked.

"Yes," Erin answered, now somewhat excited. "I just want who-ever has the most needs to be there. It's the closest to our bedroom, and it has the most space. However, if one of our other kids has more needs, let's put that child in there. In my mind, Garrison has the most needs. But if Taylor or Murphy has greater needs, they should go in the room."

Awesome. We finally had her win. She wanted whichever child had the most needs to be in that room. Now it was my turn, but the problem was that I had no idea what I wanted. Which was why I didn't want to have the conversation in front of a big group of people.

Erin started by repeating my initial solution. "Why do you want Taylor in that bedroom?"

The truth was that I didn't care which of my children were in that room. And yet I was stuck on Taylor, so obviously, I cared on some level. Erin continued asking me questions. She didn't rush me or dispute my answers. But I was lost about what I really wanted.

"Do you remember why you quickly concluded that Taylor needed to be in the new room?" Erin asked.

"Not really," I answered, confused. "I think it was right after I heard you talking to a friend about a paint color or something for Garrison's room."

And then it hit me. I instantly realized what I wanted. "I know why I was so insistent that this was Taylor's room," I explained. "I thought that you made the decision by yourself. I think I felt left out when, in my mind, you made the choice independently. I want to feel included in the decision. I want you to value my thoughts and opinions as your teammate."

Erin could have pushed back and claimed that she had tried to include me or that I had misinterpreted her actions. But she did a great job of validating what I wanted. "So if I hear you correctly," she said, "instead of me telling you which child is going into the room, you want to feel included in the decision."

"Yes!"

In the end, by using curiosity, we were able to identify the real wins for both of us:

Erin: to put whichever child has the greatest needs in the room

Greg: to be included in the decision

Does this process make sense? The next time you and your spouse are in a power struggle, I hope your automatic thought is that you're dealing with surface solutions and you need to find the real wants and desires—the hidden treasure. Once you find these nuggets, both must be factored in. That's how you get to a win-win solution. If you take what is most important to you and what is most important to your spouse and add both to the mix, you always end up with a win-win solution.

3. Seek the Lord's Opinion

I love the third step because not only does it add another layer of safety, it connects us to our Father's heart. When Erin and I pray together, we are inviting the God of this universe into our decision-making process. I can't think of a better way to foster safety in our marriage. The primary question that you are asking your heavenly Father is if He has an opinion about the decision you are trying to make. You want to put aside the desires you just identified. Don't get rid of them; just put them on the shelf for a few minutes. The reality is that if the Lord actually does have a direction He would like you to go, wouldn't His solution be the best?

It's amazing how many arguments get resolved after you ask the

Lord what He thinks you should do and seek His will for your marriage. Another way is to discuss what the Bible says about the issue. Although the Scriptures do not deal specifically with every issue you'll encounter as a couple, you are making sure that the direction you're going or what both people want does not violate biblical truth.

The best part about praying together is that when a couple kneels before the Lord and seeks His will as a team, this act instantly restores unity. Needless to say, our heavenly Father is passionate about unity: "I appeal to you, brothers and sisters, in the name of our Lord Jesus Christ, that all of you agree with one another in what you say and that there be no divisions among you, but that you be perfectly united in mind and thought" (1 Corinthians 1:10). God's desire is that we remain in unity as a *team*. Our heavenly Father explained the power of unity: "If as one people speaking the same language they have begun to do this, then nothing they plan to do will be impossible for them" (Genesis 11:6). Praying together is an outstanding way to reestablish unity.

Erin and I prayed together about the new-bedroom decision, and we didn't sense a strong leading that God wanted one particular child in that room, so we moved on to the next step.

4. Brainstorm Different Solutions

To me, this step is a blast because you get to generate a bunch of potential solutions. Have fun! The key is to allow the creative juices to flow freely. At this point, you don't want to judge or critique the ideas you generate. You do that in the next step. Here, it's important that both people have the opportunity to share ideas and suggestions. Don't forget: Any solution discussed must include both wins that you identified in step two.

Back to the new-bedroom discussion. If you remember, Erin

wanted to put whichever child had the greatest needs in the bedroom, and I wanted to be included in the decision. Using these two factors, we invited the audience to help us brainstorm solutions that contained both wins. I figured that three hundred brains were better than two—or 1.5, as my middle daughter, Murphy, claims! Right after we asked for assistance, a guy in the back of the room started frantically waving his hand. "Either you have a great idea," I joked, "or you really need to go to the bathroom."

"Why don't you guys take all decisions off the table and wipe the slate clean?" the man said. "Then sit down together and talk about what each child needs. Once you figure out who has the greatest need for the space, put that child into the room."

Let's quickly move on to the last step so we can evaluate his recommendation.

5. Pick a Solution That Feels Great to Both People, and Put It into Action

During this last step, your goal is to analyze, critique, and evaluate the ideas you generated in step four and pick the best option. If you need more input or feedback, don't hesitate to do some research on the Internet or at your local library (that's the place with all the actual books!). Talk to friends or consult an expert. Whatever you do, you need to pick the best possible solution—something that you both feel great about.

Erin and I talked briefly about the man's suggestion. It contained the things that we both wanted: Erin would get the child with the most needs in the room, and I would get to be a part of the decision. Presto! Like magic, we had a win-win solution to our conflict. Now we needed to put it into action. Try it out. Take it for a test-drive. See if it's as good as you thought it would be. But go into it with the same teammate mind-set that helped you get there in the first place—make sure both of you see it as a win-win.

Driving home from the event, Erin and I had a great conversation about what our children needed in a room. I was amazed by how deeply and thoroughly my wife understood what our kids needed. Most of what she shared, I never would have thought about in a million years. This is why I'm so thankful that God's plan for children is to be raised by a both a mother and a father. I included the "and father" part because I was able to share my perspective as well. And there were things that I perceived our children needing that Erin hadn't thought about. (I'm serious!)

When we were done talking about what our children needed, it was crystal-clear who should be in that room. After all that work, who do you think ended up in the new bedroom? The answer may surprise you!

Over the years I've asked couples at my live seminar to vote on who they thought ended up in the bedroom. Because there are many demented minds out there, I've heard plenty of crazy guesses. Here are some of my favorites:

"Rodney." No, the Ozark Mountain builder did not come to live with us.

Some people have guessed it was me. Thankfully, I didn't have to move out of my bedroom!

"Murphy." This is an interesting guess. Actually, it's the choice that receives the most votes. For those who guess Murphy, the pick is a classic example of what most of us are taught to do in this situation. Can you guess what the word is? *Compromise.* It sounds so logical, doesn't it? I wanted Taylor, and Erin wanted Garrison. Thus, put the other child into the room so no one loses.

However, I hate the word "compromise." The reason I don't like the concept is that a compromise isn't a win the majority of the time.

Sure, it may end the argument, but usually, we are left with a bitter taste in our mouth. We are left unfulfilled. It's like giving a Twinkie to a person who is starving to death. You've given him something to eat, and his belly is somewhat satisfied. But you've given him a facade—something that will never satisfy his need for real food. Erin and I went through the steps to discover something that felt great; we didn't do all the work only to settle. To me, a compromise means that you are settling for second best. A win-win means that you are finding the best—something that feels great to both people. That's what I want. What about you? Now back to the story.

In the end, it wasn't Rodney, me, or Murphy who ended up in the new bedroom. It was Garrison. Every guy reading this book is thinking, "Greg, you idiot. If you had just given your wife what she wanted in the first place, you could have been watching football this whole time!" I could have given in and placated my wife to get out of the argument. But what would that have done to my team? I hope you see that any time I feel something is a loss, my marriage team loses. Trust me. I've kept my mouth closed many times in an effort to keep the peace. It may work sometimes, but my team pays a price even if we don't realize it right away. Don't stay silent. Be strong and courageous. Speak up if something really feels like a loss for you. The truth is that after we talked about what our children needed, it was clear that Garrison had the greatest needs. By this point, however, I felt completely included in the decision. Thus, it was a win-win for me.

If you argue with a woman and win, you lose.

—AUTHOR UNKNOWN

The bottom line is that it doesn't matter who came up with the idea. What matters is that both people feel great about the decision, and you each consider it a win. There will be plenty of times when you end up doing what your spouse wanted to do originally, but by the time you get there, you will feel great about it (win-win). There will be other times when you do exactly what you suggested in the first place, but at this point, your spouse will feel great about it (win-win). And there will be times when you'll come up with a completely different solution that neither of you thought about before. In any event, the goal is always to find a solution that makes you both feel great.

WHAT IF WE CAN'T FIND A WIN-WIN SOLUTION?

Inevitably, someone always asks, "Who makes the decision if we can't find a win-win?"

Honestly, in all of the years that Erin and I have been using the win-win process, we have never run into a situation where we failed to find a solution that we both felt great about. I'm not exaggerating for dramatic effect. I'm telling you the truth. And we've had to make some major decisions, like job and career changes, moving to new cities, having more children, taking on debt, pursuing graduate school, investing our money, adoption, how to handle family crises, and so on.

We've never failed to find a win-win because the issue or topic is never the problem. I trust you are clear that the real problem always has to do with our buttons getting pushed and our true wants remaining unsatisfied. I am convinced that if you follow the above five steps, you will find something you both feel great about.

"What if we still can't find a win-win?" you contend. If this happens, my first guess would be that you didn't uncover someone's deepest desire. Don't panic or throw your hands up in defeat. Simply go back to step number two and keep digging for what it is that you both really want—what is the real win for each person? Don't worry; you'll get there.

The other question I hear often is "What if we need to make a quick decision and we don't have time to work through the steps?" If that is the reality, then you need to decide how big an issue the conflict is to you. How important is it? Is the issue high-ticket or low-ticket for you? There are times when Erin and I don't see eye to eye on a situation, and my win is to serve her and let her make the decision. Even though I might want us to go in a different direction or I would choose something else, if the issue isn't something that's high ticket or something that I want to battle over, I'll let Erin decide. My goal is to outserve my wife. However, you have to be at a place of feeling like it's truly a win for you to let your spouse make the decision. Do not stay silent, placate your spouse, keep the peace, or stuff down your feelings if what your mate is doing will feel like a big-time loss for you. If it is a high-ticket issue for you and you feel like you are losing, have the courage to say something and find a win-win.

When you let someone else win an argument, often
you both end up winners.

—RICHARD CARLSON

Let me explain something else I've discovered about these time-sensitive issues. When I'm faced with a decision that feels incredibly urgent or time-limited, my experience has been that these opportunities of a lifetime are usually misleading. Many times the opportunity doesn't turn out like it first appeared, or an even better choice has not materialized. This is why Erin and I resist making hasty decisions until we are unified. However, if a decision needs to be made fast for legitimate reasons and we haven't reached a place of unity, we will attempt to determine who is the most qualified. In any given situation, we might base that on prayer, knowledge, wisdom, experience, or training. In other situations, the deciding factor might be something else entirely. Once we figure out which one of us seems most capable, we let that person make the call. In these situations, guys, please don't pull the submit card. It's so anti-relational! Don't forget that the verse right before the infamous submission verse, Ephesians 5:21, says, "Submit to one another out of reverence for Christ." Paul is telling both spouses to submit. As the leader, a husband does not "rule over" his wife. Jesus modeled servant leadership and stated that if you want to be the leader, then you must become a servant (Matthew 20:25–28). When speaking directly to husbands, Paul instructs, "Husbands, love your wives, just as Christ loved the church and gave himself up for her" (Ephesians 5:25). Paul is telling us to follow Christ's example and "lay down our life" for our wife, as Christ did for us on the cross. Headship doesn't mean you make decisions on your own. Only a foolish leader would ignore the insights, intuition, and wisdom of his teammate. Besides, if you take on an attitude that says, "I'm the leader, so I make the decision," I guarantee your wife will feel that she has lost, and your team will lose. In the same way, women, don't suggest that your intuition or "gut" is superior. You respect your husband when you recognize that each decision may require a different set of skills, gifts, talents, wisdom, or experience and that your husband may be more qualified. Here, the goal is to discover which spouse might be better suited in a particular situation to make the best decision. That is how you submit unto each other and honor the amazing ways that God has gifted each one of you.

Whoever ends up feeling more qualified to make the quick decision, do so with great caution and humility. You may want to say something like, "I feel led to make this decision. But since you and I are not together on this, I'm acknowledging the possibility that I may make the wrong decision. Therefore, I'm making the call, but I will also take the blame if I'm wrong. I will also be the one who answers to God."

The final step in breaking the Reactive Cycle is to problem solve as teammates. Remember, Satan's primary strategy against your marriage is to divide and conquer. He wants disunity and separateness, while God desires unity and oneness. You achieve unity in your marriage when you remember that you are on the same team. Your spouse is your teammate, not your enemy. In a marriage, there is no such thing as a win-lose. Because you are married, you will either win together or lose together. There is no other option! If you need to make a decision, safety is cemented when you choose to find a solution that feels good to both of you. This win-win attitude helps to keep hearts open and enables you to create a marriage that feels like the safest place on earth. I want to leave you with one of my favorite quotes from an unknown author: "A snowflake is one of God's most fragile creations, but look what they can do when they stick together." Now imagine what you and your spouse can accomplish when you work together as a team!

Peace is costly, but it is worth the expense.

—AFRICAN PROVERB

Final Word—
Fight for Your Marriage

As the author of marriage, God created the relationship between a husband and wife to be the deepest and most intimate human connection possible. As a matter of fact, God used the word "one" to illustrate the splendor of the intimacy found in a marriage—"the two shall become one flesh" (Genesis 2:24). Marriage is about a man and a woman becoming one heart, one soul, one mind, and one body—oneness. And yet one of the greatest threats to our oneness is unhealthy conflict. Conflict will take you toward one of two destinations: intimacy or disconnection. Since conflict is inevitable and every marriage has its challenges, the true test is how you deal with them. Romans 12:18 says, "If it is possible, so far as it depends on you, be at peace with all men." No doubt these words were also intended for married couples, but I don't think Paul was talking about peace at the expense of facing our issues as a couple. It's like the famous quote by Dorothy Thompson: "Peace is not the absence of conflict but the presence of creative alternatives for responding to conflict."[1] Peace in a marriage happens not because there is no conflict; it happens when we successfully manage our differences. It's how we choose to respond to conflict that produces the growth or creates the disconnection. Peace is taking the initiative to resolve a difficult argument rather than avoid it.

Difficulties are meant to rouse, not discourage. The human spirit is to grow strong by conflict.

—WILLIAM ELLERY CHANNING

The problem is that most of us have not been taught how to effectively manage conflict. Therefore, we often shy away from an argument or don't deal with our issues openly. Instead of reaping the benefits of conflict, we try to ignore, stuff down, deny, overlook, or avoid the issues. Sadly, unresolved conflict keeps our relationship from growing and exacerbates problems. Why? Unresolved conflict is always buried alive. Our unresolved issues will continue to grow and fester until they come out in some destructive way. On the other hand, couples who face their problems may deal with some short-term discomfort and pain, but they profit more in the long run than couples who ignore conflict. As my good friend Gary J. Oliver says, "Many discuss the cost of conflict but few discuss the value of conflict. Conflict is the process we go through and the price we pay for intimacy."[2] This is the "value" of healthy conflict. Friendship, intimacy, and deep connection happen when we confront our differences, hurt feelings, frustrations, and unmet expectations in a healthy way. My hope is that this book has provided a clear vision and process for managing conflict in all of your most important relationships.

The good news is that God has an ultimate purpose in mind for marital conflict. Certainly, He wants us to reap the relational benefits of conflict, and He desires that we use conflict to better understand our spouse's feelings and needs. He definitely desires that we use our arguments to move our marriage into the deepest levels of intimacy and connection. However, 1 Peter 1:6–7 explains God's true purpose for our conflict: "In this you greatly rejoice, even though now for a little while, if necessary, you have been distressed by various trials, so that the proof of your faith, being more precious than gold which is perishable, even though tested by fire, may be found to result in praise and glory and honor at the revelation of Jesus Christ."

Here we see that our heavenly Father uses conflict to achieve eternal results. If we keep our hearts open to God, He will use our conflict to purify us as individuals, strengthen our faith, and bring honor and glory to Christ. I like how Dennis and Barbara Rainey explain it:

> God's purpose in our conflicts is to test our faith, to produce endurance, to refine us, and to bring glory to Himself. This is the hope He gives us—that we can actually approach our conflicts as an opportunity to strengthen our faith and to glorify God.[3]

This is the greatest lesson I've learned about conflict. All the times when we wrangle, clash, argue, and fight, God uses these instances to help us become conformed to His son's image. In other words, God takes these painful and frustrating moments in our marriage to make us more like Christ. Conflict is really about Christlikeness! But it's so easy to lose this eternal perspective when we are entangled in earthly conflict. The apostle Paul recognized God's ultimate purpose when he wrote, "For those God foreknew he also predestined to be conformed to the likeness of his Son, that he might be the firstborn among many brothers" (Romans 8:29).

The absence of war is not peace.

—HARRY S. TRUMAN

The real question is, how do we know if we are becoming like Jesus? Again, the good news is that we don't have to guess. Christ made it clear about how we know whether our life is being transformed in John 13:34–35: "A new commandment I give you: Love one another. As I have loved you, so you must love one another. By this all men will know that you are my disciples, if you love one another." The evidence of "Christlikeness" is in the way we love each other. One of the best ways to demonstrate a Christlike love is through how we manage conflict with others, especially with our spouse. Mahatma Gandhi gave us a beautiful picture of this goal when he said, "Whenever you are confronted with an opponent, conquer him with love."

Peace is a journey of a thousand miles and it must be taken one step at a time.

—LYNDON B. JOHNSON

Conflict helps us become like Christ. Therefore, not only do we need to be open to what God will teach us, but we must also watch with expectant eyes for the blessings He will provide during the difficult and painful times of conflict. He makes a powerful promise about what He does when we face trials: "Consider it all joy, my brethren, when you encounter various trials, knowing that the testing of your faith produces endurance. And let endurance have its perfect result, that you may be perfect and complete, lacking in nothing" (James 1:2). God will not only use conflict to grow us into His son's likeness, He will bless us in many other countless ways. Here is a reminder of what God can do through your disagreements. Healthy conflict . . .

- brings problems into the light so you can deal with them
- allows you to view your struggles as opportunities for growth
- helps you discover your spouse's deepest feelings and needs
- fuels creativity
- provides an opportunity to break old, ineffective patterns and habits
- gives you a chance to care for and empathize with your spouse
- helps you to better appreciate the differences between you and your spouse
- restores unity and oneness
- allows you to guard against being too complacent in the marriage
- draws you closer to the Lord as you deal with feeling helpless
- fosters humility, and God gives His grace to the humble
- gives you great insight into your own personal issues
- helps you learn how to anticipate and resolve future conflicts

- creates intimacy and fosters connection as you listen, understand, and validate each other
- cleanses and purifies a relationship
- reduces tension as emotions are vented and stress is released
- creates a greater sense of trust and safety if managed in healthy ways
- propels a relationship to higher levels of cooperation and teamwork
- reveals great information about your marriage in that it's telling you that something is relationally out of kilter
- raises your marriage to higher levels of satisfaction every time you manage the conflict well

You see, healthy conflict is an amazing gift and is consistent with Christ's promise to use "all things"—even conflict—for His honor and glory. "And we know that God causes all things to work together for good to those who love God, to those who are called according to His purpose" (Romans 8:28). We can always trust that God will use our conflict to grow closer to Christ and each other if we keep an open heart!

My encouragement to you is to keep short accounts. In other words, commit to dealing with conflict quickly so that you can remain in an openhearted relationship with your spouse—as well as with your children, parents, siblings, extended family, coworkers, and friends. We definitely need to follow Paul's advice:

But avoid foolish and ignorant disputes, knowing that they generate strife. And a servant of the Lord must not quarrel but be gentle to all, able to teach, patient, in humility correcting those who are in opposition, if God perhaps will grant them repentance, so that they may know the truth, and that they may come to their senses and escape the snare of the devil, having been taken captive by him to do his will. (2 Timothy 2:23–26)

Don't allow Satan to gain a victory by disconnecting you from someone you care about and closing your heart because of unhealthy or unresolved conflict.

Are you ready to embrace healthy conflict wholeheartedly? Are you willing to view healthy conflict as the doorway into the deepest levels of intimacy in your marriage? Are you prepared to stop ignoring or avoiding conflict? Instead of playing it safe, are you ready to face your marital disagreements head-on and learn how to manage them in ways that will honor God and your family? The choice is yours.

A great marriage is not when the "perfect couple" come together. It is when an imperfect couple learns to enjoy their differences.

—DAVE MEURER

But beware! Your sworn enemy will come against you and intensify your conflict. He wants to "kill, steal, and destroy" any effort to create healthy conflict in your marriage. He will increase his efforts to push your emotional buttons. He will intensify his efforts to write lies on your heart. He desperately wants you in the Reactive Cycle so that your heart will stay closed and eventually harden. But don't lose hope. You have the ability to counter with God's armor: "Finally, be strong in the Lord and in his mighty power. Put on the full armor of God, so that you can take your stand against the devil's schemes" (Ephesians 6:10–11). Your armor is what you've learned—an open heart, personal responsibility, emotional awareness, God's truth, compassion, curiosity, understanding, validation, empathy, forgiveness, and teamwork. Use these tools to fight the evil one and bring your marriage into the deepest levels of intimacy and connection.

———————

While you are proclaiming peace with your lips, be careful to have it even more fully in your heart.

—ST. FRANCIS OF ASSISI

———————

If you chose to walk through the doorway of conflict, you and your spouse are in for an amazing ride. You have the opportunity to experience a depth of intimacy you may have never experienced before—safety, trust, passionate connection, and deep friendship are waiting for you on the other side of conflict. Keep on fighting for your marriage!

May the Lord make your love increase and overflow for each other and for everyone else, just as ours does for you. May he strengthen your hearts . . . (1 Thessalonians 3:12)

Acknowledgments

This book could not have been completed without the help of family, friends, and colleagues.

Thank you to my children, Taylor, Murphy, Garrison, and Annie, who have always cared about and supported my heart and passion—thanks for the special gift of being your father.

Thank you to Nicci Jordan Hubert, an exceptionally gifted writer, for being my editor.

Thank you to Andrea Jewell for the exceptional editorial assistance.

Thank you to Lee Hough of Alive Communications for his outstanding help in bringing this project to reality.

Thank you to my colleagues at Focus on the Family for your support in the writing of this book.

Thank you to the counselors at the National Institute of Marriage.

Thank you to Howard Books and Philis Boultinghouse for your partnership and bringing my passion for married couples to life.

Acknowledgments

And, finally, thank you to the Howard Books and Simon & Schuster teams who have engaged in copyediting, internal design and layout, cover design, and the myriad of details required to bring this book to press.

Notes

CHAPTER 1

1. Dallin H. Oaks, "World Peace," *Ensign* (May 1990), https://ccr.byu.edu/quickquotes/peace (accessed May 13, 2012).

2. Howard J. Markman, Scott M. Stanley, and Susan L. Blumberg, *Fighting for Your Marriage: A Deluxe Revised Edition of the Classic Bestseller for Enhancing Marriage and Preventing Divorce* (New York: Jossey-Bass, 2010), 4.

3. Thomas F. Crum, *The Magic of Conflict: Turning a Life of Work into a Work of Art* (New York: Simon & Schuster, 1998), 31.

4. Larry Alan Nadig, "Relationship Conflict: Healthy or Unhealthy," *Guidelines for Effective Communication*, http://www.drnadig.com/conflict.htm (accessed May 13, 2012).

5. John Gottman, "John Gottman on Couples Therapy," *Psychotheraphy.net* (July 2000), http://www.psychotherapy.net/interview/john-gottman (accessed May 13, 2012).

6. John Gottman, *Why Marriages Succeed or Fail: And How You Can Make Yours Last* (New York: Simon & Schuster, 1995), 28.

7. Nadig, http://www.drnadig.com/conflict.htm.

8. Gottman, *Why Marriages Succeed or Fail: And How You Can Make Yours Last*, 173.

9. Gary Oliver, Center for Relationship Enrichment, "Growing Through Conflict," http://liferelationships.com/resources/articles/viewarticle.asp?article id=277&categoryid=33 (accessed May 13, 2012).

10. John Gottman, Gottman Relationship Institute, "Gottman's Top Relationship Tips," http://www.gottman.com/49804/Self-Help-and-Tips.html (accessed May 13, 2012).

11. Gary Smalley, *Secrets to Lasting Love: Uncovering the Keys to Lifelong Intimacy* (New York: Fireside, 2000), 94–95.

CHAPTER 2

1. Robert Burney, Joy2meu, "Codependent Relationships Dynamics," http://www.joy2meu.com/codependent1.htm (accessed May 13, 2012).

2. John Gottman, *The Seven Principles for Making Marriage Work* (New York: Crown, 1999), 132–133.

3. LifeScript, "Don't Let Your 'Hot Buttons' Spoil Your Chances," http://www.lifehack.org/articles/communication/don't-let-your-"hot-buttons"-spoil-your-chances.html (accessed May 13, 2012).

4. J. H. Larson, "The Marriage Quiz: College Students' Beliefs in Selected Myths About Marriage," *Family Relations* (1988): 37, 3–11.

5. Lauren Papp, Mark Cummings, and Marcie Goeke-Morey, "For Richer, for Poorer: Money as a Topic of Marital Conflict in the Home," *Family Relations* (February 2009), 58, 100.

CHAPTER 3

1. John Eldredge, *Waking the Dead: The Glory of a Heart Fully Alive* (Nashville: Thomas Nelson, 2006), 34.

2. Shad Helmstetter, *What to Say When You Talk to Your Self* (New York: Simon & Schuster, 1982), 22.

3. John and Stasi Eldredge, *Love & War* (New York: Doubleday, 2009), 29.

4. Holley Gerth, Heart to Heart, "Out of Insecurity 5: I Have a Confession," http://www.holleygerth.com/heart-to-heart-with-holley/2010/2/23/out-of-insecurity-5-i-have-a-confession.html (accessed May 13, 2012).

5. Steven Curtis Chapman and Mark Hall, "Voice of Truth," Casting Crowns, Beach Street Records, 2003.

CHAPTER 4

1. Lizette van Huyssteen, Practically Speaking, "Amygdala Hijacking," http://practicaprogram.blogspot.com/2010/09/amygdala-hijacking.html (accessed May 13, 2012).

2. Ibid.

3. Ibid.

4. Relly Nadler, "What Was I Thinking? Handling the Hijack," *True North Leadership* (July 2009), http://www.psychologytoday.com/files/attachments/51483/handling-the-hijack.pdf (accessed May 13, 2012).

5. Ibid.

6. Ibid.

7. Katherine Kam, "Rein in the Rage: Anger and Heart Disease," *WebMD* (May 2007), http://www.webmd.com/heart-disease/features/rein-in-rage-anger-heart-disease (accessed May 13, 2012).

8. Howard J. Markman, Scott M. Stanley, and Susan L. Blumberg, *Fighting for Your Marriage: A Deluxe Revised Edition of the Classic Bestseller for Enhancing Marriage and Preventing Divorce* (New York: Jossey-Bass, 2010), 23.

9. John Gottman, *Why Marriages Succeed or Fail: And How You Can Make Yours Last* (New York: Simon & Schuster, 1995), 104.

10. Neil Rosenthal, "The Signs of Gridlock," *Heart Relationships* (2010), http://heartrelationships.com/article/signs-gridlock-part-1 (accessed May 13, 2012).

CHAPTER 5

1. Kristie Karns, eHow, "How Does a Shark Smell Blood from Miles Away?" http://www.ehow.com/how-does_4579345_shark-smell-blood-miles-away.html (accessed May 18, 2012).

2. "Memorable Quotes for *Inception*," www.imdb.com/title/tt1375666/quotes (accessed May 18, 2012).

3. Les and Leslie Parrott, *I Love You More* (New York: Zondervan, 2005), 59.

4. John and Stasi Eldredge, *Love & War* (New York: Doubleday, 2009), 95.

5. Some of the lies can be found at the following websites: http://www.maryvillemoms.com/marriage-2/top-10-lies-satan-tells-about-marriage/; http://marlothomas.aol.com/2010/09/15/top-10-myths-about-marriage-and-how-to-get-over-them/.

6. http://www.cbn.com/family/marriage/ferwerda_lies-affairs.aspx?option =print. Used by permission.

7. Eldredge, *Love & War*, 95.

8. Wikipedia, "The Matrix," http://en.wikipedia.org/wiki/The_Matrix (accessed May 18, 2012).

CHAPTER 6

1. Adam Pick, *The Patient's Guide to Heart Valve Surgery* (Heart Valve Interactive Corp., 2012), http://www.heart-valve-surgery.com/heart-surgery-blog/2010/04/11/open-close-each-day/.

2. Krishna Madu, "Animals Self Protection," July 19, 2009, Shvoong.com, http://www.shvoong.com/exact-sciences/zoology/1914819-animals-self-protection/#ixzz1oFMxQU00.

3. Adam Anderson, Leavitt Institute, "A Heart Condition" (accessed May 18, 2012).

4. Cindy Beall, *Healing Your Marriage When Trust Is Broken: Finding Forgiveness and Restoration* (Harvest House Publishers), 86.

5. Casting Crowns, "Slow Fade" (admin. by EMI CMG Publishing, 2007), My Refuge Music/Club Zoo Music/SWECS Music (BMI).

6. http://www.midlife-men.com/mid-life-crisis-affair.html. Used by permission.

7. http://faithfull4him.wordpress.com/2011/02/28/cure-for-a-hardened -heart. Used by permission.

8. Greg Smalley and Shawn Stoever, *The Wholehearted Marriage* (Howard Books, 2009), 27.

9. Max Lucado, *Thoughts About God*, "Hard Hearted," http://thoughts-about-god.com/blog/2011/02/19/ml_hard-hearted/ (accessed May 18, 2012).

10. http://talkaboutmarriage.com/general-relationship-discussion/12734-apathy -marriage.html. Used by permission.

11. Doug Apple, *Apples of Gold*, "Marriage Key: Soften Your Heart," www.wak ulla.com/Community/Community_Columnists/Apples_of_Gold_(by _Doug_Apple):_Marriage_Key;_Soften_Your_Heart_200805135246/ (accessed May 18, 2012).

12. Ed Price, *The Loving Heart* (2002), http://www.surfinthespirit.com/advice/ open-your-heart.shtml.

13. Smalley and Stoever, *The Wholehearted Marriage*, 28.

14. Wayne Blank, The Church of God, "The Tearing of Clothes," www.keyway. ca/htm2007/20070313.htm (accessed May 18, 2012).

15. Lucado, "Hard Hearted."

CHAPTER 7

1. John Gottman and Nan Silver, "What makes marriage work?" *Psychology Today* (October 1, 2009), http://www.psychologytoday.com/articles/200910/ what-makes-marriage-work.

2. Max Lucado, *When God Whispers Your Name* (Nashville: Thomas Nelson, 1994), 44.

3. James Groesbeck with Amy Swierczek, *The First Five Years of Marriage* (Colorado Springs, CO: Focus on the Family, 2006).

4. http://www.theinstituteforhumandevelopment.com/Articles/Personal-Growth/AspectsofSelfsoothing/tabid/127/Default.aspx.

5. John Gottman, *Why Marriages Succeed or Fail: And How You Can Make Yours Last* (New York: Simon & Schuster, 1995), 117, 178.

6. Karen Sherman, "Give Me Space!" *Hitched*, http://www.hitchedmag.com/ article.php?id=284.

7. Karla McLaren, *Emotional Genius: How Your Emotions Can Save Your Life,* http:// www.lightworksav.com/browseproducts/EMOTIONAL-GENIUS—HOW-YOUR-EMOTIONS-CAN-SAVE-YOUR-LIFE—(8-CD-SET). HTML.

8. Vaughn, MindHacks, "Labeling Emotions Reduces Their Impact," www. scn.ucla.edu/pdf/Mind Hacks_AL.pdf (accessed May 14, 2012).

9. www.mdjunction.com/forums/borderline-personality-discussions/general -support/984907-naming-emotions. Used by permission.

CHAPTER 8

1. Gary J. Oliver and Carrie Oliver, *Mad About Us: Moving from Anger to Intimacy With Your Spouse* (Ada, MI: Bethany House, 2007).

2. Archibald D. Hart and Sharon Hart Morris, *Safe Haven Marriage: Building a Relationship You Want to Come Home To* (Nashville: Thomas Nelson, 2003), 28.

3. John and Stasi Eldredge, *Love & War* (New York: Doubleday, 2009), 37.

4. Barbara DeAngelis, *What Women Want Men to Know* (New York: Hyperion Books, 2001), 117.

5. Dinah Craik, *A Life for a Life* (University of California Libraries, 2011), 270–271.

6. Merriam-Webster.com, "Honor," http://www.merriam-webster.com (accessed May 18, 2012).

7. Marriage Missions International, "Communication and Conflict," www.marriagemissions.com/quotes-on-communication-and-conflict/ (accessed May 14, 2012).

8. Ibid.

9. Sara Paddison, *The Hidden Power of the Heart* (Boulder Creek, CA: Heartmath, 1998).

10. Psychology Wiki, "Compassion," http://psychology.wikia.com.

11. Steven Stosny, "Anger in Marriage: Failure of Compassion and the Rise of Contempt," *Psychology Today* (Nov. 4, 2009), http://www.psychologytoday.com.

CHAPTER 9

1. Momentum Coaching, "Personal Listening Profile," www.momentum-coaching.com/personal_listening_profile.html (accessed May 14, 2012).

2. Merriam-Webster.com, "Listening," http://www.merriam-webster.com (accessed May 18, 2012).

3. H. Norman Wright, *Communication: Key to Your Marriage* (Ventura, CA: Gospel Light, 1979), 95.

4. David G. Benner, *Sacred Companions: The Gift of Spiritual Friendship & Direction* (Downers Grove, IL: InterVarsity Press, 2002), 52.

5. Howard J. Markman, Scott M. Stanley, and Susan L. Blumberg, *Fighting for Your Marriage* (New York: Jossey-Bass, 2001).

6. David Olson, Amy Olson-Sigg, and Peter Larson, *The Couple Checkup* (Nashville: Thomas Nelson, 2008).

7. Compiled from information found on http://eqi.org/invalid.htm.

8. Steve Hein, EQI.org, "Validation and Invalidation," http://eqi.org/eqe96_5.htm (accessed May 18, 2012).

9. A. Mehrabian, *Silent Messages: Implicit Communication of Emotions and Attitudes* (Belmont, CA: Wadsworth, 1981).

10. Michael McMillan, "What Meaning Do Your Words Carry?" (2012), http://www.michaelmcmillan.com/what-meaning-do-your-words-carry.

11. Elizabeth Bernstein, "I'm Very, Very, Very Sorry. . . Really?" *Wall Street Journal,* http://online.wsj.com/article/SB10001424052702304410504575560093884004442.html (accessed October 18, 2012).

12. Ibid.

13. Peter J. Larson, *New Forgiveness Research* (Jan. 27, 2003).

14. J. Oranthinkal and A. Vansteenwegen, "The effect of forgiveness on marital satisfaction in relation to marital stability," *Contemporary Family Therapy* (2006), 28, 251–260.

15. F. Beach, S.R.H. Fincham, and J. Davila, "Longitudinal relations between forgiveness and conflict resolution in marriage," *Journal of Family Psychology* (2007), 21, 542–545.

CHAPTER 10

1. Robert Alan Silverstein, "Better World Quotes," *People for Peace Project,* http://www.betterworld.net/quotes/win-win-quotes.htm (accessed May 14, 2012).

FINAL WORD

1. Dorothy Thompson, http://en.wikipedia.org/wiki/Dorothy_Thompson.

2. Gary Oliver, "Conflict: Friend or Foe?" Back to the Bible, The Good News Broadcasting Association, Inc. (Lincoln, Nebraska, all rights reserved, 2012), http://www.backtothebible.org/conflict-friend-or-foe.html.

3. Dennis Rainey, *Staying Close* (Nashville: Thomas Nelson, 1989), http://www.familylife.com/site/apps/nlnet/content3.aspx?c=dnJHKLNnFoG&b=3577191&ct=4639663&notoc=1.